A TEN-YEAR STUDY

THE K-8 Principal IN 1988

By
James L. Doud

D1096853

*Sixth in a Series of
Research Studies Launched
in 1928*

National Association of Elementary School Principals

Library of Congress Catalog Card Number: 89-60293

Copyright 1989
National Association of Elementary School Principals
1615 Duke Street, Alexandria, Virginia 22314-3483

Printed in the United States of America

Table of Contents

List of Tables

List of Figures

Foreword

In my 35 years as an educator, I have witnessed and experienced many changes in the principalship. A lot of them have been changes for the better: principals today certainly enjoy more prestige, higher salaries, and greater authority than they did when I was a rookie.

But some of the changes have been troubling. We don't see so many of those nice, easy-to-teach, middle-class children from the old "Ozzie and Harriet" show in our classrooms. And we don't see Ozzie and Harriet on Parents' Night, either. What we do see are steadily rising numbers of at-risk children, including some who do not speak English as a first language, who need all the educational help we can give them. We see almost one child in four coming from a single-parent household and one in six going home each day to a home where no adults are present.

This latest NAESP ten-year study documents a decade of changes and establishes a fresh statistical base on which to measure the changes that will most certainly manifest themselves between now and 1998, when we will again do a comprehensive study of the principalship.

It is enlightening to compare the findings of this 1988 study with those of 1978, a year marked by declining enrollments, staff reductions, and school closings. Budgets were tight, salaries were modest, and there was little enthusiasm for educational innovations. Of the 13 top problems ranked by principals that year, number one was getting rid of incompetent staff.

And then along came the tidal wave of educational reform, beginning with the publication of *A Nation At Risk* in 1983. Suddenly a harsh spotlight focused on our schools. Change became the order of the day.

Public education has taken a lot of heat over the last five years, but the elementary school principalship has emerged not only unscathed but enhanced. Research has proven that the common denominator for effective elementary schools is an effective principal. Today's principal is better educated and better prepared than ever before. The old image of the deskbound administrator and disciplinarian is being replaced by a new and more fitting image as an instructional leader more concerned with improving teaching than devising bus schedules. It is significant that the principals surveyed for this study listed unsatisfactory student performance as their top problem.

Perhaps the greatest change in the elementary school principalship over the last ten years is one that will become even more pronounced and significant in the next ten years. It is school-based management, arising from the growing realization that principals can do a better job of instructional leadership when given adequate decision-making authority. Almost three-quarters of the principals surveyed in 1988 noted they were included in administrative teams established by the central office to make decisions concerning their schools. Nine of ten principals rated their level of authority as "high" or "moderate."

There is still a long way to go. Less than half of the surveyed principals felt that they had been given appropriate control over the school or the hiring of teachers. If they are to have responsibility for supervising and evaluating teachers, the reasoning goes, they should also be responsible for hiring them.

The principal of the 1990s faces enormous challenges that may affect the very structure of the elementary school. But if this survey is an indicator, the men and women who will take on that challenge will have the training, the tools, and the power to do the job.

Samuel G. Sava
Executive Director, NAESP

Preface

This 1988 survey of the elementary/middle school principalship is the sixth of its kind, with similar studies having been conducted in 1928, 1948, 1958, 1968 and 1978. Together they provide both a running account of the factors that affect the status of the K-8 principal and a perspective of the societal changes that have shaped American education during the past 60 years and that continue to be of concern to principals in 1988. A few of the issues bearing on the status of the principalship have remained constant in each of the studies. Many are of course sharply different, particularly those that confront the principal in 1988.

The past decade, and especially the five years since the publication in 1983 of *A Nation At Risk* by the National Commission on Excellence in Education, has been marked by perhaps the most concentrated attention that American education has ever received. The 1983 report was quickly followed by a series of additional "national reports," each driven by the desire to promote a particular point of view and all calling for improvement of the educational system so that the United States might more effectively compete in the "information age" and in a global economy. As North Carolina's former Governor James B. Hunt, Jr., said in a report of the Task Force on Education for Economic Growth:

> "Nothing matters more—nothing. Education is the public enterprise in our country that is closest to people's hearts—and most important to their lives. And education is the enterprise that is crucial to success in everything we attempt as a nation."

In the day-to-day conduct of the education enterprise, this surge of public interest has brought far wider awareness of the crucial importance of the principal's leadership in the life of a school. The impact of this heightened awareness on the elementary or middle school principal's job was one of the issues NAESP sought to explore in this study.

Like its five predecessors, the study is aimed primarily at practicing principals. It is an attempt to identify conditions principals deal with as they go about their business of providing leadership to their school's instructional program.

The raw data generated by the survey are far more extensive than could be addressed in this document. In determining what information to include, the author has attempted to keep in mind the primary audiences for which the report is intended: practicing school principals (plus those aspiring to become principals) and persons involved in educational research and history.

J.L.D.

Scope and Limitations of the Study

An eight-page survey instrument containing 84 questions was mailed in the spring of 1987 to 2,414 principals. Rather than focusing only on NAESP members, the participants were randomly selected from a list of all public schools that included any of the grades from K through 6 (with the exception of K-12 schools). Thus principals both in schools focusing on the middle grades and in early childhood centers—as well as the more traditional K-4, K-6, and K-8 structures—were included. A follow-up study was mailed to the total sample, with 834 responses received. This represents a rate of response of 34.5 percent.

The responses to each question were tabulated during the summer and fall by the Educational Research Service. Tabulations were provided for the total sample as well as for each of the following subgroups:

- Years of experience (less than 5; 5 to 14; 15 or more)
- Size of school (less than 400; 400 to 600; more than 600)
- Community type (urban; suburban; small town; rural)
- Sex (male; female)
- NAESP member (yes 5 years or less; yes more than 5 years; no)
- Age (40 or less; 41 to 50; older than 50)
- Would become a principal again if starting over (certainly/probably would; certainly/probably would not)
- Elementary principalship as final goal (yes; no)
- Degree status (bachelor's/master's; sixth year/Ph.D.)

These tabulations generated nearly 250 pages of data, the

highlights of which are reported in this publication. Where available and appropriate, comparative data from previous studies are provided also.

Since the information in the study was gathered through a sampling, it is of course subject to sampling variation. It is important that the possible variation be kept in mind when attempting to draw inferences about the universe of all principals working in public schools that include any grades K-6 (except K-12) schools. It should also be considered when attempting to compare the responses of two groups of respondents (e.g., male and female principals) and then to generalize answers to the two respective populations. Information about how to estimate the amount of sampling variation associated with population inferences drawn from sampling percentages contained in this report is included in the technical note of the Appendix.

Chapter 1

Personal Characteristics of Principals

A s the research on effective schools demonstrates "the principal is the one individual who is directly involved in every aspect of the school's operation, and therefore is the primary figure in determining the school's quality and character," (NAESP *Standards for Quality Elementary Schools*, p. 7).

In examining how that responsibility is being carried out, this report focuses attention first on the personal and professional characteristics of today's elementary and middle school principals.

What is your title?

Principals today are full-time administrators.

The title now applied to most elementary and middle school principals reflects the continuation of a trend noted during the past 20 years toward recognition of the elementary school principalship as a full-time administrative position. The extent of the change that has taken place is indicated by the fact that just 30 years ago the unmodified title of "principal" (as contrasted with, say, "teaching principal") was not even used in the NAESP survey.

In the current study, terms such as "supervising principal" (one of the most common of the previously used designations) have given way to today's almost universally accepted "principal." As seen in Table 1, the percentage of respondents reporting "principal" as their title rose to 96.4 percent, an increase of 3.7 percent from the 1978 study and 27.4 percent from 1968. Meanwhile the incidence of another

1

TABLE 1—POSITION TITLE

Titles	1968	1978	1988
Principal.....................	69.0%	92.7%	96.4%
Supervising Principal..........	12.6	1.1	N.D.
Teaching Principal.............	14.6	3.7	1.1
Head Teacher..................	3.8	0.5	N.D.
Supt./Prin. or Supt.	N.D.	N.D.	1.4
Asst. Supt./Prin./Asst. Supt.......	N.D.	N.D.	0.2
Other........................	N.D.	2.0	0.8

variant, "teaching principal," has steadily declined (14.6 percent in 1968; 3.7 percent in 1978; 1.1 percent in 1988). Other titles reported in the current survey include "superintendent/principal" or "superintendent" (1.4 percent), "assistant superintendent/principal" or "assistant superintendent" (.2 percent), and "other central office/principal" or "other central office" (.8 percent).

More than 96 percent of the respondents to this survey have no teaching responsibilities (see Table 2). When teaching responsibilities *were* reported (in combination with administrative duties) such positions were found almost exclusively in schools with enrollments of less than 400 students. The mean amount of time devoted to teaching by principals who do teach is 36 percent of the school day. Although teaching principals may be found in all types of communities, a careful analysis of data indicates that they work primarily in small schools or small school districts, generally supervise fewer than ten teachers, and in very small districts may hold the title of "principal/superintendent."

What is your age?

The typical K-8 principal is 47 years old.

The median age of all principals in this survey—and the median also for men—is 47 years (Table 3). The median age for women principals is two years younger (45). These 1988 figures reflect continuation of a trend that has consistently narrowed the gap in median ages between men and women principals, and this is the first NAESP ten-year study to indicate women as being the younger of the two groups.

TABLE 2—PERCENT OF ADMINISTRATOR TIME ASSIGNED TO CLASSROOM TEACHING

| | Total | Size of School | | | Community Type | | | | | Sex | |
		Less than 400	400-600	More than 600	Urban	Sub-Urban	Small Town	Rural	Male	Female
Have no teaching responsibilities	96.5%	91.8%	99.7%	100%	96.3%	99.0%	96.5%	93.8%	97.3%	93.5%
Have teaching responsibilities	3.5	8.2	0.3	0.0	3.7	1.0	3.5	6.2	2.7	6.5
Mean..................	36	37	01	00	36	21	42	33	27	49

TABLE 3—MEDIAN AGE OF PRINCIPALS (YEARS)

Year	Total	Sex	
		Male	*Female*
1928	N.D.	43.4	48.5
1948	46.5	44.4	50.0
1958	47.6	43.7	52.0
1968	46.0	43.0	56.0
1978	46.0	45.0	49.0
1988	47.0	47.0	45.0

It is noteworthy that the youngest principal reported in this study was a 27-year-old female.

The age distribution (Table 4) documents that the percent of females under 40 years of age is 8.5 percent higher than that reported in 1978, while the percent of males in this same category decreased by 9.1 percent. Although progress in bringing more women into the elementary principalship may be slower than desired, inroads *are* being made, notably in the appointment of younger women. Should the conditions reflected in this study continue, one might expect the next ten-year study to reflect a more dramatic increase in the percentage of women holding elementary and middle school principalships.

What is your sex?

Recent years have seen concerted efforts across the country to promote and implement affirmative action in equal op-

TABLE 4—AGE DISTRIBUTION OF PRINCIPALS

Age Group	Total	Sex			
		Male		Female	
		1978	*1988*	*1978*	*1988*
under 35.........	4.7%	13.1%	4.2%	5.7%	6.7%
35-39	16.3	16.5	16.3	9.1	16.6
40-44	21.7	16.3	22.3	18.1	19.6
45-49	19.2	20.9	18.1	18.1	23.3
50-54	19.9	18.8	20.2	21.8	18.4
55-59	13.5	10.0	14.0	16.1	11.7
60 or more.......	4.7	4.5	5.0	11.1	3.7

portunity employment policies and practices. The study shows that such programs have had a positive impact on the employment of women during the past 15 years (though not, as will be further noted later, on the employment of minorities of race). The representation of women in the principalship is now 20.2 percent, an increase of 2.2 percent during the past ten years (see Table 5). The trend in that direction is most evident when comparing the sex of principals with less that five years of experience (see Figure 1), in which category 40.4 percent of the principalships are held by women. This is the highest percentage of female representation in the principalship since the 1928 study, when 55 percent of the elementary school principals were reported to be women. Women principals are found in all sizes of schools and communities, although the data indicate that they are more likely to be found in schools of less than 400 students (22.1 percent) and in urban areas (where they constitute 26.5 percent of the principals).

Table 6 documents that the balance of female-to-male principals varies from one region to another across the United States. There are four regions in which more than one of every four principals is likely to be female: the Southwest (29.3 percent), New England (28 percent), the Southeast (27.4 percent), and the Far West (25.3 percent). The regions reporting the lowest percentage of female principals are the Great Lakes (9 percent), the Rocky Mountains (12.5 percent), the Plains (14.6 percent), and the Mideast (21.7 percent).

How would you place yourself among (the following) racial or ethnic groups?

The white male continues to represent the "typical" K-8 principal.

The historic preponderance of whites in the principalship (currently 89.8 percent) continues unabated, as Table 7 demonstrates. Though the overall number of Hispanic principals remains relatively small, their representation has shown an increase (3.5 percent in 1988 compared to .9 percent in 1978). However, the percentage of black principals (4.4 percent) has declined by 1.1 percent during the past ten years. Within gender groups, the percentage of black females (8.3 percent) is more than twice as high as the percentage of black males (3.5 percent). Minority principals

TABLE 5—GENDER OF PRINCIPALS

| | Total | Size of School | | | Community Type | | | |
		Less than 400	400-600	More than 600	Urban	Sub-Urban	Small Town	Rural
Male	79.8%	77.9%	82.1%	80.3%	73.5%	80.7%	84.7%	79.8%
Female	20.2	22.1	17.9	19.7	26.5	19.3	15.3	20.2

TABLE 6—SEX OF PRINCIPALS BY REGION

Region	Total	Male	Female
New England	5.2%	4.7%	7.2%
Mideast............	13.8	13.6	15.0
Southeast..........	20.2	18.4	27.5
Great Lakes........	24.8	28.3	11.4
Plains	10.8	11.4	7.8
Southwest	9.8	8.7	14.4
Rocky Mountains...	3.8	4.2	2.4
Far West	11.5	10.7	14.4

States included in regions—*New England*: CT, MA, ME, NH, RI, VT; *Mideast*: DE, DC, MD, NJ, NY, PA; *Southeast*: AL, AR, FL, GA, KY, LA, MS, NC, SC, TN, VA, WV; *Great Lakes*: IL, IN, MI, OH, WI; *Plains*: IA, KS, MN, MO, NE, ND, SD; *Southwest*: AZ, NM, OK, TX; *Rocky Mountains*: CO, ID, MT, UT, WY; *Far West*: AK, CA, HI, NV, OR, WA.

FIGURE 1—SEX OF RESPONDENT BY YEARS EXPERIENCE IN THE PRINCIPALSHIP

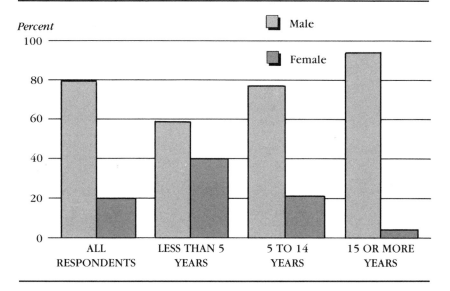

tend to be concentrated in urban communities, where approximately two of 11 principals are members of a minority. They are least likely to be found in rural communities, where the ratio is approximately one of 15. With a rapidly increasing minority population, particularly in the major cities—and with well-documented demographic studies

TABLE 7—RACIAL OR ETHNIC COMPOSITION OF ELEMENTARY PRINCIPALS

	Total	Urban	Community Type			Sex	
			Sub-Urban	Small Town	Rural	Male	Female
Hispanic	3.5%	6.3%	2.0%	3.5%	2.2%	3.3%	4.2%
Native American ...	2.2	1.1	3.5	1.6	2.8	2.6	.6
Asian/Pacific Isl. ...	0.0	0.0	0.0	0.0	0.0	0.0	0.0
Black	4.4	11.1	2.0	3.1	1.7	3.5	8.3
White.............	89.8	81.0	92.5	91.8	93.3	90.5	86.9
Other Nonwhite ...	0.1	0.5	0.0	0.0	0.0	0.2	0.0

projecting that by about the year 2010 one of every three Americans will be black, Hispanic, or Asian American (Harold Hodgkinson, *Principal*, January 1986, p. 11)—the current imbalance in the percentage of minorities in the principalship indicates an urgent need for greater efforts to recruit minorities into school leadership positions. Programs of equal opportunity employment and affirmative action appear to be having only a modest impact on the situation.

How would you classify yourself in regard to your basic political philosophy?

Politically, principals tend to be a bit conservative.

This question evoked fewer responses (748) than any other in the survey. Possible explanations for this reluctance to respond include: 1) a long-standing feeling by elementary principals that they should remain out of political "involvement"; 2) hesitance by principals to publicly identify themselves with one "side" or the other; 3) failure to define the response terms; and 4) the tendency of individuals to move from one political orientation to another according to particular issues. Nearly 80 percent of the respondents (See Table 8) declared themselves to be politically in the middle; that is, they either "tend to be conservative" (53.6 percent) or "tend to be liberal" (26.3 percent).

When the two conservative response categories are combined, principals in the current study appear to differ little in political philosophy from those who participated in the 1978 study. Nearly seven of ten elementary and middle school principals (69.6 percent) place themselves in the

TABLE 8—BASIC POLITICAL PHILOSOPHY OF ELEMENTARY PRINCIPALS

Political Philosophy	Total	Community Type				Sex		Degree Status	
		Urban	Sub-Urban	Small Town	Rural	Male	Female	Bach/Mast	6-Yr/Ph.D.
Conservative	16.0%	14.4%	17.0%	15.2%	18.1%	17.4%	11.0%	16.7%	14.4%
Tend to be conservative	53.6	43.7	55.9	61.0	50.3	55.3	47.4	54.7	51.5
Tend to be liberal	26.3	37.1	22.9	22.1	25.2	24.8	31.8	25.3	28.4
Liberal	4.0	4.8	4.3	1.7	6.5	2.5	9.7	3.3	5.7

9

political right, a figure that is just 1.6 percent less than that reported ten years ago. Within genders, nearly three out of four men (72.7 percent) and about three out of five women (58.4 percent) continue to identify themselves in the "conservative" categories—figures that are very consistent with those reported a decade earlier.

Looking at the combined "liberal" response categories, the principals who consider themselves liberal are most frequently found in urban (41.9 percent) and rural (31.7 percent) areas, contrasted with the less than 24 percent in small towns. The 31.7 percent figure for rural principals reflects a rather marked change, as only 23 percent identified themselves as liberal in 1978. Although the differences are very small, the percentage of "liberal" appears to increase slightly with level of education.

At what age (approximately) are you planning to retire from the principalship?

Plans for retirement confirm the prospect of high turnover.

Much has been reported in the professional literature to indicate that the nation's schools will soon be hit by an unusually high turnover in the principals. Some observers have predicted that this turnover will exceed 50 percent by 1992. The timing of the 1988 study thus provided a good opportunity to try to gauge the realities of the situation.

The years between ages 62 and 68 have traditionally been seen as the "normal" years for people to retire, and in fact the study shows (see Table 9) that 25.9 percent of the nation's K-8 principals plan to adhere to that custom. However, two other retirement-age levels seem to be gaining in popularity. Just over 20 percent of today's principals plan to retire at age 60 or 61 (an increasingly common level in many career fields today). Perhaps more surprising, an additional one in five K-8 principals plans to retire at age 55, and the mean expected retirement age for *all* K-8 principals is now 58 years. This development may well reflect the decision by several state governments to permit employees to retire at age 55 without penalty, if the retiree has completed a certain number of years of service—an arrangement that seems to have great appeal. All in all, the study appears to support the predictions of sizable turnovers.

TABLE 9—APPROXIMATE AGE OF PLANNED RETIREMENT FROM THE PRINCIPALSHIP

Age	Total
Less than 50	3.7%
50	2.8
51	1.8
52	4.9
53	2.3
54	1.5
55	20.6
56	3.3
57	5.0
58	5.0
59	3.0
60	19.4
61	0.8
62	10.7
63	1.8
64	0.5
65	10.8
More than 65	1.9
Mean	58

Please indicate your anticipated year of retirement.

Most of today's principals will have left by the year 2000.

More specifically, the study indicates that nearly 30 percent of the nation's K-8 principals expect to retire by 1992 (see Table 10). By 1995, this figure will have increased to 42.6 percent, and at the time of the next NAESP ten-year study in 1998, the turnover may be expected to have reached 56 percent. By the turn of the century, two of every three of today's elementary and middle school principals will have been replaced.

A word of caution about dealing with these retirement statistics: When one looks at the mean age at which three different age groups plan to retire, some interesting figures emerge that could pull down the overall retirement age re-

TABLE 10—ANTICIPATED YEAR OF RETIREMENT

Year	Total	Accumulated Total
1987	2.9%	
1988	4.7	
1989	4.4	
1990	6.9	
1991	4.0	
1992	6.9	29.8%
1993	5.4	
1994	3.4	
1995	4.0	42.6
1996	2.5	
1997	6.1	
1998	4.8	56.0
1999	3.4	
2000	5.8	65.2
2001 or after	34.9	100.1

ported in this study. Principals who are 40 years of age or less indicate they plan to retire at age 55; those who are between 41 to 50 years of age plan to retire at age 58; and those older than 50 believe they will retire at age 60. These responses suggest that it would not be surprising if the interest in early retirement displayed by today's younger principals were to fade a bit as they grow older.

At any rate, the retirement figures suggest excellent job prospects for people aspiring to become elementary or middle school principals. They also pose some complex problems for the institutions involved in preparation programs, and for local, state, and national school administrator associations. The next few years will offer an unparalleled opportunity to develop a close linkage between school and university personnel. Such partnerships could result in better identification of potential candidates for the principalship, a more acute focusing of energies and resources on developmental programs for aspiring principals, and the development of preservice and inservice principal preparation programs and activities specifically geared to the community's special needs.

SUMMARY

The elementary school principalship today is occupied by a full-time administrator who is better educated than were his counterparts in previous years. The median age of the principals in the study is 47 years. Although males continue to predominate in this role, the number of females has increased to 20 percent during the past decade.

The presence of nearly 90 percent Caucasians in the principalship makes recruitment of minorities a critical need, in the interests both of the schools and of the larger society. The next decade will offer particularly useful and pertinent opportunities to address this issue, since more than half of today's principals are slated to retire during this time span, with the mean projected age for retirement being 58 years.

Politically, nearly eight of ten principals say they fall somewhere between "conservative" and "liberal," although the clear majority is to be found in the conservative half of the continuum.

Chapter 2

Professional Characteristics of Principals

Studies focused on school administrators have characterized K-8 principals as being possessed of high energy and enthusiasm, high morale, and high satisfaction in their position.

The data in this chapter cast further light on that proposition and on the background and professional attitudes to be found among today's K-8 principals.

Do you hold membership in NAESP and/or other professional associations?

K-8 principals are dedicated to strengthening the profession.

Among the traits that consistently distinguish outstanding principals are their dedication to their profession and their interest in strengthening the principalship—both of which they demonstrate through their participation in professional associations whose activities directly relate to working in schools. Thus two of the "quality indicators" found in the *Standards for Quality Elementary Schools* speak to the following: 1) The principal actively pursues a program of professional development on a yearly basis; and 2) The principal is a member of local, state, and national professional associations and actively participates in their work.

About 47 percent of the respondents to the study are current members of the National Association of Elementary School Principals (see Table 11), a 1.1 percent increase over the figure in the 1978 study. However, there is a bit of a problem with that comparison. At the time of the 1978 Study, NAESP was beginning to experience a decline in

TABLE 11—CURRENT MEMBERSHIP AND YEARS OF EXPERIENCE AS A PRINCIPAL

Organization	Total	Years Experience		
		Less Than 5	5- 14	More Than 15
NAESP 46.7%	45.0%	45.5%	50.7%	
NASSP 15.4	17.0	16.0	13.6	
NEA 14.2	12.3	13.3	15.1	
AFT 0.2	0.0	0.3	0.4	
AASA 5.9	5.8	6.0	5.1	
ASCD 39.1	43.9	44.2	29.0	
State Admin. Assoc.	67.0	64.3	66.7	69.5
Local Prof. Admin. Assoc.	52.9	43.3	54.7	56.6
Local Admin. Barg. Union	11.7	11.7	9.5	15.1
Lcl.Tchr./Admin. Barg. Union	2.3	1.8	3.0	1.8
Other	18.8	22.2	19.0	15.1

membership—from a high of approximately 28,000 members in the mid 1970s to a low of fewer than 14,000 by 1981. Since that date, memberships have increased by nearly 10,000 (an increase of over 70 percent during the past seven years) and the current total NAESP membership exceeds 24,000.

Only state (67 percent) and local (53 percent) associations of administrators attract a higher percentage of principals than does NAESP. As regards other national professional associations, 15.4 percent of the respondents belong to the National Association of Secondary School Principals; 14.2 percent to the National Education Association (about half the 1978 figure); and 39.1 percent (including 44.1 percent of NAESP members) to the Association for Supervision and Curriculum Development.

Just over half of the women in the survey (51.2 percent) belong to NAESP, compared to 45.4 percent of the men (see Table 12). Women also are much more likely than men to hold membership in the Association for Supervision and Curriculum Development (55.4 percent to 34.7 percent) and to belong to the American Association of School Ad-

TABLE 12—MEMBERSHIP IN NATIONAL ORGANIZATIONS, BY GENDER

Organization	Sex	
	Males	Females
NAESP	45.4%	51.2%
NASSP	17.4	7.1
NEA	14.7	11.9
AFT	0.0	1.2
AASA	5.0	8.3
ASCD	34.7	55.4

ministrators (8.3 percent to 5.0 percent). On the other hand, men (17.4 percent) are more than twice as likely as women (7.1 percent) to join NASSP. It is difficult to know what to make of such data. Is it possible that women place a greater emphasis on supervision and curriculum development than men do? Are women more likely than men to see central office positions as a career option? Are more men than women interested in career possibilities at the secondary school level?

 Regardless of whether you are currently a member of NAESP, have you ever been a member?

Some 62 percent are or have been NAESP members.

Nearly 62 percent of the respondents indicated that they either are or have been NAESP members (see Table 13). This figure may speak well for *them* but may also provoke questions about the commitment of the 38 percent of K-8 principals who are strangers to their national professional association.

While fewer males than females say they have never been a member of NAESP (36.6 percent), a greater percentage of females report being *current* NAESP members (51.2 compared to 45.4 percent).

Commitment to the profession—as evidenced by membership in NAESP—appears to grow with experience. Thus it may be distressing but not altogether surprising to note that 52.7 percent of the principals reporting less than five years of experience have never been NAESP members. The nonmember percentage drops to 40.1 percent for those

TABLE 13—PRINCIPALS WHO ARE NOW, OR HAVE BEEN, MEMBERS OF NAESP

NAESP	Total	Years Experience			Community Type				Sex		
		Less than 5	5 to 14	15 or More	Urban	Sub-Urban	Small Town	Rural	Male	Female	Non-Member
Yes......	61.9%	47.3%	59.9%	76.3%	64.7%	66.5%	60.9%	56.8%	63.4%	55.8%	30.4%
No.......	38.1	52.7	40.1	23.7	35.3	33.5	39.1	43.2	36.6	44.2	69.6

18

with five to 14 years of experience and continues to fall thereafter with each rise in experience level.

The typical length of time that NAESP members have *been* members (see Table 14) is eight years (nine years for men, five for women), one year more than the mean in 1978. The overall length of membership by individuals ranges from one year to 34. Nearly one in three members say they have belonged to NAESP for three years or less, while 3.2 percent have been members for more than 25 years.

If you are currently a member, does your school district pay all or part of your dues?

More and more districts are paying dues for association membership.

More and more school systems are recognizing the value of membership in a professional association such as NAESP—a proposition demonstrated by a continuing increase in the number of school districts that pay the dues involved. Nearly 42 percent of the principals in this study (see Table 15) say their district pays *all* of their dues (an increase of 18.2 percent from 1978), and another 5.2 percent say their district pays part of the dues (up 1.5 percent).

The district covers the entire cost for more than half of the principals in rural areas (50.6 percent) and small towns

TABLE 14—YEARS OF NAESP MEMBERSHIP
(61.9% of Respondents provided "Years of Membership" data)

| Years as NAESP Member | Total | Sex | |
		Male	Female
1 to 3	30.3%	26.8%	47.2%
4 to 9	34.2	34.8	32.6
10 to 14	18.1	18.5	14.6
15 to 19	7.9	9.0	3.4
20 to 24	6.1	7.0	2.2
25 to 29	2.0	2.5	0.0
30 or more	1.2	1.5	0.0
Mean	08	09	05
Range—Low	01	01	01
High	34	34	22

TABLE 15—PAYMENT OF NAESP DUES BY SCHOOL DISTRICT

| | Total | Community Type | | | | Sex | |
		Urban	Sub-Urban	Small Town	Rural	Male	Female
District pays none of my dues	53.1%	82.8%	52.1%	38.2%	44.3%	50.8%	62.4%
District pays 100% of my NAESP dues	41.7	13.8	40.6	56.9	50.6	44.1	31.8
District pays part of my NAESP dues	5.2	3.4	7.3	4.9	5.1	5.0	5.9
Respondents	386	87	96	123	79	299	85

(56.9 percent), but only 13.8 percent of the principals in urban communities receive such support. This is a somewhat surprising result, given the number of urban principals covered by collective bargaining and the fact that payment of professional dues is one of the areas for which such bargaining is allowed. The fact that women principals are more likely to be found in urban areas may also help explain why women are about 12 percent more likely than men to be responsible for paying their own dues. At any rate, payment by the district of all or part of the professional membership dues of elementary and middle school principals is continuing to gain acceptance. This benefit has become even more attractive with recent changes in the federal tax laws that make deduction of professional dues much more difficult.

Suppose you were starting out all over again, would you want to become an elementary school principal?

Most K-8 principals are glad they are K-8 principals.

The great majority (83.6 percent) of elementary and middle school principals are evidently glad they chose that calling. If they were starting their careers over again, 50.5 percent of them would "certainly" make the same choice (see Figure 2), while another 33.1 percent would "probably" do so—responses that are consistent with the findings of the

1968 and 1978 studies. Comparing the "certainly" responses for men versus women, more women seem to be satisfied with their jobs (54.9 percent) than men (49.5 percent).

FIGURE 2—SUPPOSE YOU WERE STARTING OUT ALL OVER AGAIN, WOULD YOU WANT TO BECOME AN ELEMENTARY SCHOOL PRINCIPAL?

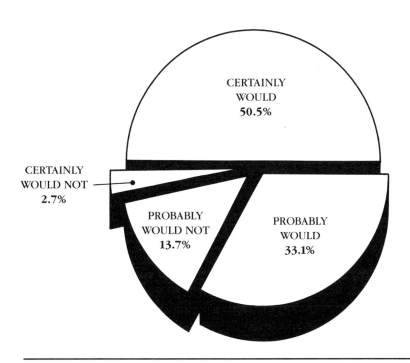

How about the relationship between level of education and interest in becoming a principal again—does more education lead to less interest? Apparently not; the responses within each category (see Table 16) reflect very little difference between principals who have a bachelor's or master's degree and those with a Ph.D.

TABLE 16—WILLINGNESS TO AGAIN BECOME A PRINCIPAL, BY DEGREE STATUS

	Total	Bach/Mast	6-Yr/Ph.D.
Certainly Yes	50.5%	51.3%	48.1%
Probably Yes	33.1	33.1	34.2
Probably No	13.7	13.1	14.4
Certainly No	2.7	2.5	3.3

Do you consider the elementary/middle school principalship your final occupational goal?

More than half of today's K-8 principals plan career shifts.

More than half of today's K-8 principals (54.4 percent) do not see their present job as representing their final career goal (see Table 17), though the great majority (84.3 percent) do want to remain in education. Those most interested in staying in the same kind of assignment as their present one (just under 50 percent) are characteristically to be found in small town and suburban schools enrolling from 400 to 600 students.

Among those indicating that the elementary and middle school principalship is *not* their final occupational goal, the greatest deviation from the 1978 responses occurred among respondents with less than five years of experience. In 1978, 63 percent of such principals felt that they had found their professional niche. By 1988 this total had dropped to only 23.2 percent. Just over 73 percent of this group aspire to become a superintendent (33.1 percent) or an associate/assistant superintendent (15 percent) or either take some other central office position (12.9 percent) or become a director of elementary education (7.3 percent).

At least three explanations for such shifts in career goals seem plausible. First, for those who have recently entered the administrative career path, there may be a driving interest in the greater income and broader influence they perceive as going with higher positions in the school system hierarchy. Since this group also includes the highest percentage of women in the principalship, a second reason may lie in greater accessibility to central office positions. A third possible explanation for a redirection of career goals

TABLE 17—FINAL OCCUPATIONAL GOAL OF ELEMENTARY SCHOOL PRINCIPALS

	Total	Years Experience			Community Type				Sex		Degree Status	
		Less than 5	5 to 14	15 or More	Urban	Sub-Urban	Small Town	Rural	Male	Female	Bach/-Mast	Ph.D.
Elementary School Principalship as Final Goal:												
Yes	45.6%	23.2%	39.8%	66.5%	43.4%	49.5%	49.6%	36.1%	46.3%	43.3%	50.1%	36.0%
No	54.4	76.8	60.2	33.5	56.6	50.5	50.4	63.9	53.7	56.7	49.9	64.0
If No, Final Occupational Goal:												
Elem. School Teacher ...	2.1	0.8	2.9	1.2	0.0	1.0	4.1	2.8	2.4	1.1	2.6	1.3
Sec. School Teacher	0.5	0.0	1.0	0.0	0.0	0.0	0.0	1.9	0.6	0.0	0.4	0.7
College Teacher	12.6	13.7	12.0	12.8	14.3	10.1	13.0	12.3	12.1	13.8	13.0	12.5
Sec. School Principal ...	3.5	1.6	3.4	5.8	1.0	9.1	1.6	2.8	3.8	2.3	4.4	2.0
Supt. of Schools	28.0	33.1	33.2	8.1	18.4	32.3	24.4	37.7	31.3	16.1	23.7	35.5
Assoc./Asst. Supt. of Schools	15.0	20.2	12.0	14.0	20.4	16.2	14.6	9.4	13.9	19.5	14.4	15.1
Dir. of Elem. Ed.	6.1	7.3	5.8	5.8	8.2	7.1	4.9	4.7	4.7	11.5	7.0	4.6
Other Central Office Personnel	10.0	12.9	10.1	5.8	14.3	5.1	11.4	9.4	9.1	13.8	11.5	7.2
Pos. Outside Field of Education	15.7	8.1	12.5	34.9	11.2	13.1	19.5	17.0	17.1	9.2	16.3	14.5
Other	6.5	2.4	7.2	11.6	12.2	6.1	6.5	1.9	5.0	12.6	6.7	6.6

would pertain primarily to those who have been on the job for several years. With a number of state retirement programs now encouraging such principals to retire at an earlier age than has heretofore been customary, many may well be looking at lucrative career opportunities outside education that were not alternatives ten years ago.

As Table 18 shows, there is a significant connection between remaining in the principalship and level of education. Principals who hold the bachelor's or master's degrees are about evenly split in the matter. Not surprisingly, however, only about a third of those who have a sixth year of education or a doctorate see the principalship as their final career goal. When considered along with the data reported in Table 16, it would appear that the attainment of a higher level of education may tend to lead a person out of the principalship but has little or no impact upon the individual's level of satisfaction while in that position.

Among the respondents who contemplate other occupational goals, the position of superintendent of schools attracts 28 percent of the total and an even greater proportion (35.5 percent) of those with a sixth year of education or the doctorate. Another 31 percent of the total respondents seek other central office positions, and slightly more than 22 percent opt for some other field (including 15.7 percent who indicate a position outside education). These percentages are nearly equal for both men and women, although a greater percent of men (31.3 percent) than women (16.1 percent) seek the superintendency, while a greater percent of women (44.8 percent) than men (27.7 percent) seek other central office positions. College teaching is an attractive final occupational goal for 12.6 percent of those who expect to leave the principalship before retirement.

TABLE 18—THE ELEMENTARY SCHOOL PRINCIPALSHIP AS A FINAL
CAREER GOAL, BY DEGREE STATUS

	Total	Bach/Mast	6-Yr/Ph.D.
Is the Principalship your final goal?			
Yes	45.6%	50.1%	36.0%
No	54.4	49.9	64.1

How would you best describe your morale?

*Morale runs
high in the K-8
principalship.*

Elementary and middle school principals are a generally satisfied, contented group, as Table 19 reveals. Nine out of ten note that their morale is either "excellent" (38.9 percent) or "good" (51.2 percent). However, slightly more than one in 100 principals do report that their morale is low.

These percentages are nearly identical within and across each of the analysis categories: experience, size of school, community type, sex, membership in NAESP, age, career goals, and degree status. "Excellent" morale is found most frequently among principals in schools of 400 to 600 enrollment and in suburban districts. Incidentally, the percentage of females expressing "excellent" morale is about 4 percent higher than that of males.

The extent of respondents' morale compared with their educational level is reported in Table 20.

How many total years (including your years as a principal) have you been employed as a professional in education?

*The typical K-8
principal has 22
years of school
experience.*

Nearly half of the respondents in the study (44.5 percent) have from 20 to 29 years of experience in the education profession (see Table 21), with the median being 22, two years more than in 1978. It may be noted that another drop in median years of experience is to be expected in the 1998 study, given the number of principals who plan to retire during the next few years.

As would be expected, the lowest median number of years of professional experience (16) was of course reported by those principals with less than five years of experience. The highest median (26 years) was reported by principals who identified the principalship as their final career goal. For principals in rural areas the median is 18 years. The median for women principals is 20, that for men is 23. No one in the sample reported fewer than four years of professional experience.

TABLE 19—MORALE OF PRINCIPALS

| Morale | Total | Size of School | | | Community Type | | | | | Sex | |
		Less than 400	400-600	More than 600	Urban	Sub-Urban	Small Town	Rural	Male	Female
Excellent ...	38.9%	36.5%	42.1%	37.4%	40.3%	43.1%	39.0%	33.7%	38.1%	42.0%
Good	51.2	51.0	49.2	55.1	50.0	50.0	50.6	52.8	51.4	50.0
Fair	8.6	11.3	7.7	5.3	8.1	5.9	9.6	11.2	9.1	6.8
Poor	1.3	1.2	1.0	2.1	1.6	1.0	0.8	2.2	1.4	1.2

TABLE 20—COMPARISON OF PRINCIPAL MORALE, BY DEGREE STATUS

Morale	Total	Bach/Mast	6-Yr/Ph.D.
Excellent	38.9%	38.2%	39.6%
Good	51.2	51.7	50.6
Fair	8.6	8.7	8.6
Poor	1.3	1.4	1.2

TABLE 21—TOTAL YEARS OF EMPLOYMENT AS A PROFESSIONAL IN EDUCATION

Number of Years	1968	1978	1988
9 or less	13.3%	7.0%	2.4%
10-19	40.3	38.4	36.8
20-29	18.6	43.6	44.5
30 or more	27.7	11.0	16.3
Median years employment	18	20	22

How many years did you teach before becoming a principal or teaching principal?

The mean number of years as a teacher is seven.

NAESP holds that persons entering the principalship should have at least five years of elementary classroom teaching experience—for good reason. As noted in *Proficiencies for Principals* (p.3): "Even the best preparation programs ... do not provide a level of practical understanding and skill comparable to that gained from working directly with students in the classroom on a day-to-day, sustained basis."

Although the mean number of years of elementary teaching experience for K-8 principals in general is reported to be a healthy 7.7 years, it is disturbing to note that 22.3 percent have had no elementary teaching experience at all (see Table 22) and an additional 8.8 percent have taught for only one or two years.

How old were you when you were appointed to your first principalship?

Nearly three of every four respondents in the survey became a principal between the ages of 26 and 39, with the

TABLE 22—TEACHING EXPERIENCE PRIOR TO BECOMING A PRINCIPAL

Level	Total	Male	Female
Elementary Teaching:			
None	22.3%	25.5%	9.8%
1 year	3.0	3.6	.6
2 years	5.8	6.6	2.5
3 years	7.3	7.7	5.5
4 years	6.4	7.0	4.3
5 years	9.4	10.2	6.1
6 to 9 years	21.6	23.2	15.3
10 or more years	24.3	16.2	55.8
Mean years taught	7.7	6.7	11.2
Secondary Teaching:			
None	58.3%	53.3%	78.1%
1 year	3.4	3.6	2.5
2 years	4.8	5.5	1.9
3 years	4.4	4.9	2.5
4 years	3.1	3.4	1.9
5 years	2.8	3.1	1.3
6 to 9 years	10.9	12.4	5.0
10 or more years	12.4	13.8	6.9
Mean years taught	7.2	7.2	7.1

mean starting age being 34 (see Table 23). Gender made a difference. The mean age at which men first became principals was 33; for women it was 39. Over 30 percent of the men were principals by age 29, contrasted with 10 percent of the women. Nearly half (45.7 percent) of the women received their first appointment to the principalship after age 40, while 13.9 percent of the men were appointed at a similar age. Interestingly 5 percent of the respondents first became principals at age 25 or less (5.6 percent of the men and 2.5 percent of the women).

The study reveals a gradual increase in the age at which principals are appointed to their first principalship. For principals with 15 or more years of experience, the mean age is 32; for those with five to 14 years, the mean is 34 years; and for less than five years, it is 39.

TABLE 23—AGE AT TIME OF FIRST APPOINTMENT AS PRINCIPAL

Age Group	Total	Sex		Years Experience		
		Male	Female	Less Than Five	5-14	15 or More
Less than 26	5.0%	5.6%	2.5%	3.0%	3.3%	8.9%
26-29	21.1	24.5	7.4	3.6	20.3	33.6
30-34	30.3	33.2	18.5	18.5	34.8	31.4
35-39	23.5	22.7	25.9	34.5	22.5	18.1
40-44	10.4	8.3	19.1	17.3	10.1	5.9
45-49	7.0	4.7	16.7	15.5	6.8	1.8
50 or older	2.7	0.9	9.9	7.7	2.2	0.4
Mean age	34	33	39	39	34	32

Given the probability that the next ten years are likely to see increased numbers of retirements, not to speak of continued progress in affording equal opportunities to women and to minority groups, the 1998 study of the principalship will likely show a downward trend in the mean age at which principals—men and women alike—first *become* principals, and the men vs. women disparity in age when first appointed will also diminish.

 Was an assessment center available to you prior to your selection for your position as a principal?

Assessment centers seem unknown to all but a few principals.

A fairly recent trend in the process of selecting principals has been the advent of assessment centers. Although a variety of such assessment operations are becoming available, the one most frequently cited is the NASSP-developed Principal's Assessment Center model, which uses six activities as the basis for assessing a candidate's abilities in 12 generic administrative skill areas. The growth of assessment centers has mushroomed since 1981; at the time of this study there were about 50 centers in 37 states, plus two overseas and one in Canada.

Despite this rapid growth, only 6 percent of the respondents report being aware of their availability (see Figure 3). Twenty percent did not know whether such a center was available, and 74 percent said one was *not* available. Many

FIGURE 3—ASSESSMENT CENTER AVAILABLE PRIOR TO
YOUR SELECTION AS PRINCIPAL

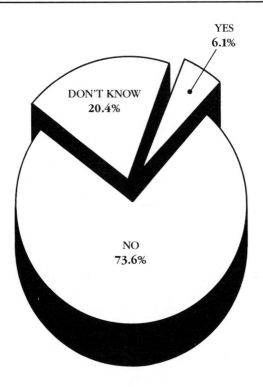

YES
6.1%

DON'T KNOW
20.4%

NO
73.6%

of the persons included in this study have been in the principalship longer than five years, and thus no assessment
center would have been available to them.

Of the 6 percent of the respondents for whom an assessment center was available, nearly two-thirds (62.5 percent)
participated in this process. Such a participation rate—
combined with the rapid expansion in the number of assessment centers, the practice by some states of mandating
their use, and the projection of a large turnover in the principalship during the next decade—appears to assure continued growth in the use of some type of skills assessment
process as a part of future principal selection procedures.

Counting this year, how many years have you been principal of your current school?

The typical time at the current school is five years.

The typical K-8 principal has been in his/her current school for five years, the same figure that was reported in both 1968 and 1978 (see Table 24). For women the median length of time is only three years, whereas for men it is six years.

Nearly 37 percent of K-8 principals are within their first three years in that position, a typical probationary period. An additional 37.6 percent are in their 4th to 9th year and 21.3 percent are in their 10th to 19th year, with 4.2 percent having held that position for at least 20 years. Overall, the tenure of nine out of ten women and seven of ten men is less than ten years.

Have you ever served as a principal in another school district?

K-8 principals seem to be an exceptionally stable group.

The overwhelming majority of K-8 principals (71.7 percent) have never served as a principal in a different school district than the one they are in now (See Table 25). Of the 28.3 percent who *have* been a principal in another district, two-thirds of them have served in just one additional district, one in five has worked in two districts, about one in ten has worked in three districts, and 2.8 percent have served in four or more. Males (32.9 percent) are about three times as likely as females (10.3 percent) to have worked in another district.

TABLE 24—YEARS, INCLUDING CURRENT YEAR, AS PRINCIPAL IN CURRENT SCHOOL

Years	1968 Total	1978 Total	1988 Total	Sex Male	Sex Female
Three or fewer	37.6%	34.1%	36.7%	32.5%	54.0%
4-9	32.4	42.7	37.6	37.9	36.2
10-19	23.1	19.7	21.3	24.2	9.2
20 or more	6.9	3.5	4.2	5.1	0.6
Median	5	5	5	6	3

TABLE 25—PRINCIPALS WHO HAVE SERVED IN OTHER SCHOOL DISTRICTS
(28.3% of Total Population)

| | | Community Type | | | | Sex | |
	Total	Urban	Sub-Urban	Small Town	Rural	Male	Female
Total of Sample	28.3%	13.0%	25.2%	36.2%	36.5%	32.9%	10.3%
One other district	65.9	60.9	67.4	69.9	59.3	64.0	88.2
Two other districts	21.5	26.1	17.4	20.5	25.4	22.8	5.9
Three other districts	9.8	13.0	10.9	7.2	11.9	10.2	5.9
More than three other districts	2.8	0.0	4.3	2.4	3.4	3.0	0.0

The data also reflect a direct relationship between principal stability and the type of community involved. In general, the bigger the community, the smaller the turnover in K-8 principals. Only 13 percent of the principals in urban districts have served as principals in another district, while about 25.2 percent of suburban principals and slightly more than 36 percent of the principals in small town and rural districts have worked in at least one other district.

If yes, have you ever served as a principal in another state?

K-8 principals tend to stay where they are.

About one in five of the respondents who have worked in more than one school district (see Table 26) have also served as a principal in another state. (Cautionary note: The actual number of responses reflected in this table is only 48 (6 percent), and of these 48 respondents, only 8 (16.7 percent) report working as a principal in two or more other states. Somewhat surprisingly, nearly half (47.1 per-

TABLE 26—PRINCIPALS WHO HAVE SERVED IN OTHER STATES
(6.0% of Total Population)

| | | Sex | |
	Total	Male	Female
Principals who served in another state	21.1%	19.0%	47.1%

cent) of the women who have worked in some other school district, also have worked in a different state. This figure among males is only 19 percent.)

Clearly, elementary and middle school principals tend to be stabile; they are not given to moving about.

Counting this year, how many years have you been a school principal altogether?

The typical K-8 principal has been in that job for 11 years.

The typical K-8 principal today has been in that job for 11 years, a longevity increase of one year over the finding in 1978 and the highest figure ever reported in this series of ten-year studies (see Table 27). For women the median is five years and for men 12, a disparity that is not as great as it may seem, given the increasing number of women who have become K-8 principals during the past decade.

Meanwhile there has been a slight increase (1.2 percent) over the 1978 figure in the number both of principals with three or less years of experience and those with 20 or more (4.7 percent), a reversal of declines reported in 1978 (see Table 28). Of the 17.9 percent of respondents who have been in the principalship for at least 20 years, 6.9 percent have been principals for 25 years or more, suggesting that those who speak about the "graying of the principalship" may have a point.

TABLE 27—MEDIAN YEARS OF EXPERIENCE AS A PRINCIPAL

							Sex	
	1928	*1948*	*1958*	*1968*	*1978*	*1988*	*Male*	*Female*
Median	10.1	10.5	9.1	9.0	10.0	11.0	12.0	5.0

TABLE 28—TOTAL YEARS AS A PRINCIPAL

Years	*1968*	*1978*	*1988*
1-3	22.3%	15.4%	16.6%
4-9	30.1	33.8	29.4
10-19	31.6	37.7	36.0
20 or more	16.0	13.2	17.9

SUMMARY

More than half of the nation's elementary and middle school principals belong to their state and local administrator organizations, and just under half are members of NAESP. Nearly half of the NAESP member principals report that all or part of their dues to the association are paid by the school district.

Elementary and middle school principals are highly satisfied with their position, as evidenced by the fact that 85 percent say they would either "certainly" or "probably" make the same career choice if starting over again, and that about 90 percent say their morale is either "excellent" or "good."

K-8 principals tend to be stabile, with less than 30 percent reporting they have worked in more than one district or in more than one state. The mean length of time spent in the principalship is 11 years. Although less than half of the respondents see the K-8 principalship as their final career goal, this appears to be more a matter of striving than of dissatisfaction with the principalship.

The median number of years that today's principals have served as education professionals is 22, including some classroom teaching. Their median age when they were first appointed to the principalship is 34. By sex the median is 39 for women and 33 for men, a disparity that seems destined to rapidly narrow.

Chapter 3

Professional Preparation of Elementary and Middle School Principals

F ormer Secretary of Education William Bennett won considerable attention during the three and a half years he served in that post by advancing a number of propositions that were at a minimum off-beat. One of them was his theory that specific preparation for the principalship was not really necessary—that the schools could turn to retired army officers, for example, or maybe businessmen looking for a change of scenery. In some states, moreover, the idea seemed to perhaps be catching on; there has been much talk in New Jersey, for example, about minimizing the certification requirements for principals and teachers alike.

NAESP, which has long held that the qualifications for being a K-8 principal should include at least three years of experience as a teacher, was struck by Dr. Bennett's notion and wondered how general it was. Thus the 1988 survey included the following:

 Does your state require a specific certification for principals?

Most states require that principals possess proper certification.

The responses showed that, as of now at least, the Bennett idea is at best localized. Nearly 95 percent of the respondents reported the existence of specific state certification requirements for principals (see Table 29). Further, about half of the states represented by the respondents also have

TABLE 29—STATE CERTIFICATION REQUIREMENTS FOR PRINCIPALS

	Total
Yes	94.6%
No	5.4
If yes, are there re-certification requirements?	
Yes	49.9
Every Year	2.1
Every 2 Years	2.6
Every 3-4 Years	21.7
Every 5 Years	52.7
Every 6 Years or More	13.4
No information provided on time period	7.5
Mean years before re-certification	**5.0**
No	41.4
Don't know/no response	8.6

requirements for *recertification* every five years, and another 26 percent require recertification within the first to fourth years of service.

To date, then, few states would appear to have taken up Dr. Bennett's notion but rather are in effect in support of the NAESP position. As expressed in such publications as *Standards for Quality Elementary Schools* and *Proficiencies for Principals*, NAESP endorses not only specific preparation and certification but also a requirement that principals be continuously engaged in professional development activities that keep them up to date and knowledgeable about current developments in the field.

What certifications do you currently hold in the state in which you're working?

By far, most principals today are certified as principals.

Nearly 94 percent of the survey respondents hold certification as a principal (see Table 30), and nine out of ten also hold state certification as a teacher, with women (95.7 percent) being slightly more likely than men (88.7 percent) to be in this latter group. One in three respondents hold certification as a superintendent or administrator or supervisor.

TABLE 30—STATE CERTIFICATIONS CURRENTLY HELD BY PRINCIPALS

		Sex		Degree Status		Final Goal	
Principalship	Total	Male	Female	Bach/ Mast	6-Yr Ph.D.	Yes	No
Teacher	90.1%	88.7%	95.7%	90.6%	89.2%	89.4%	90.5%
Principal	93.9	93.7	94.5	93.2	95.4	93.6	94.0
Superintendent	33.9	36.7	23.2	23.6	57.5	26.3	40.9
Other Admin. or Supervisor	34.1	31.5	44.5	30.9	41.7	31.3	36.3

(Multiple certification is probable and accounts for percent totals which exceed 100 in each category)

Men (36.7 percent) are more likely than women (23.2 percent) to hold certification as a superintendent, but 44.5 percent of the women held certification as "other administrator or supervisor," compared to just 31.5 percent of the men. This response to the certification question reflects a historical pattern by which women who manage to rise in central office positions have had to settle for something less than the superintendency (AASA, 1985). In recent years, however, there has been a slow but steady move toward naming women to the system's top position, and the traditional sex disparities in central office positions seem bound to diminish during the next ten years.

Level of education also plays a role in the types of certification reported by the respondents. Those with bachelor's or master's degrees are much less likely to hold certification as a superintendent (or other administrative position) than are those who have completed a sixth year or doctoral program. While such a finding seems only natural, since certification programs are based primarily upon completion of additional coursework, the data contain a surprise. It turns out that of those who hold the necessary credentials for top-level positions, twice as many choose to remain K-8 principals (or at least not seek certification for a higher position) than those who *do* seek such certification. One possible interpretation of this development is the proposition that more and more educators see K-8 schooling as such a crucial level of education that it represents their terminal career option. If that analysis be true, there would appear to be an increasing need for specialized graduate school offerings for career K-8 principals.

What is the highest college degree (excluding honorary degrees) you hold?

The master's degree is just about standard for today's K-8 principal.

Nearly seven out of ten elementary principals (68 percent) hold the master's degree as the highest degree earned (see Table 31). Two percent hold only a bachelor's degree, while nearly 30 percent indicate completion of a six-year certificate or doctoral degree program. Over 31 percent of the women (including 13.8 percent with doctoral degrees) and just under 30 percent of the men (including 8.7 percent with doctorates) hold a degree beyond the master's.

Those persons appointed as principals before age 30 are about four times as likely to have had "some" advanced work as they are to hold the master's degree. Another bulge is evident within the 40 to 44 age group, where 29.5 percent report completing at least one year of advanced study (compared to 18.5 percent with the master's degree). With the exception of the 50 to 54 age group, where the percent of persons holding the master's degree is 5.4 percent higher than that reported for more advanced study, the proportion of principals who have completed at least six years of study versus those with just a master's degree are within 4 percent of one another.

In 1928 approximately 15 percent of K-8 principals held at least a master's degree. By 1948 (no study was done in 1938), the proportion had soared to no less than 64 percent—in effect making a master's the standard for the K-8 principalship. The "normal" academic preparation for the

TABLE 31—DEGREES HELD BY ELEMENTARY PRINCIPALS

| | Total | Sex | |
		Male	Female
Bachelor's	2.1%	2.3%	1.2%
Master's	68.0	68.1	67.7
Six-Year Certificate	20.2	21.0	17.4
Doctorate	9.7	8.7	13.8

principalship today is clearly at least the master's degree (see Figure 4) and the level continues to climb.

Current efforts to extend the preparation of *teachers* beyond the bachelor's degree will doubtless mean greater pressure on principals to achieve at least the six-year certificate and, increasingly, to complete doctoral studies.

How many of the following positions have you held?

The big majority of principals started out in the classroom.

As the responses to this question show, the men and women who hold elementary and middle school principalships bring to that post a broad variety of educational experiences and backgrounds. The vast majority had been teachers prior to taking their first principalship—65.4 percent at the elementary level, 40.8 percent at the intermediate level, and 35.6 percent at the secondary level (see Table 32). Women were more likely than men (82.6 percent vs. 60.9 percent) to move into a principalship directly from elementary-level teaching. Men were twice as likely as

FIGURE 4—HIGHEST DEGREE HELD

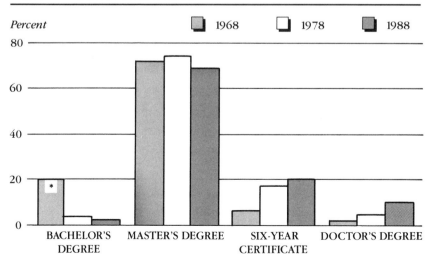

*Includes less than Bachelor's

TABLE 32—POSITIONS HELD BY PRINCIPALS

Before First Principalship

	Total	Sex Male	Sex Female
Elementary Teacher	65.4%	60.9%	82.6%
Intermediate Teacher	40.8	42.1	35.9
Secondary Teacher	35.6	39.7	19.8

Before Current Principalship

	Total	Sex Male	Sex Female
Elementary Teacher	68.2%	63.4%	86.8%
Intermediate Teacher	43.2	44.5	38.3
Secondary Teacher	37.7	42.1	20.4

(Multiple teaching positions are probable and account for percent totals which exceed 100%.)

women to have had secondary teaching experience, three times as likely to have been a secondary level assistant principal, and about 23 times more likely to have been a coach (27.8 percent) than were women (1.2 percent). The image of the "retired" coach from the secondary school who becomes the elementary or middle school principal, at one time a fairly common practice in some parts of the country, appears to be fading; today only 22.4 percent of the total group report this background.

An assistant principalship was the route to their first principalship for slightly more than one in ten of the respondents, with 15.6 percent reporting that experience. For about 6 percent the path to the principalship lay through counseling or college teaching, and for 7.4 percent it was experience as a central office administrator. Women were slightly more likely than men to have experience as a counselor, and twice as likely to have been a member of a college faculty. The responses were much the same (though with slightly higher percentages in each category) when the principals were asked about their experience prior to their current assignment—including teaching experience at each level, coaching, an assistant principalship (20 percent have served as assistant principals in elementary schools), counseling, college teaching, and central office administration.

What has been the value of the following types of preparation and experience to your becoming a successful elementary school principal?

Nothing compares with on-the-job experience, the participatants in the survey say.

With this question the respondents were asked to rate the value of nine different kinds of preparation and experience to their success as a principal. The responses inevitably had to arise from personal, individual experience, resulting in wide variations in the number of responses reported for each item.

K-8 principals see on-the-job experience as a principal (96.8 percent), experience as a teacher (83.4 percent), and experience as an assistant principal (66.7 percent) as having "much value" to their success as a principal (see Table 33). Graduate education, inservice study and training, and meetings of local/state principals have "much value or some value," according to more than 90 percent of the respondents. The respondents clearly spoke from firsthand knowledge: About 53 percent had *been* assistant principals, and more than 85 percent had had each of the other experiences.

TABLE 33—VALUE OF TYPES OF PREPARATION AND EXPERIENCE
TO SUCCESS AS ELEMENTARY PRINCIPAL

	Total
On the job experience as principal: (94.2% of respondents reported participating: N = 786)	
Of much value	96.8%
Of some value	2.8
Of little value	.4
Experience as a teacher: (96.6% of respondents reported participating: N = 806)	
Of much value	83.4
Of some value	15.3
Of little value	1.2

TABLE 33—CONT.

Experience as an assistant principal:
(52.8% of respondents reported participating: N = 440)

Of much value	....	66.7
Of some value	....	12.2
Of little value	....	21.0

Graduate education:
(93.5% of respondents reported participating: N = 780)

Of much value	....	35.8
Of some value	....	57.0
Of little value	....	7.2

Inservice study and training:
(85.9% of respondents reported participating: N = 716)

Of much value	....	35.5
Of some value	....	54.5
Of little value	....	10.0

Local/state meetings of principals:
(88.7% of respondents reported participating: N = 740)

Of much value	....	23.5
Of some value	....	59.3
Of little value	....	17.3

Internship in elementary school administration:
(45.6% of respondents reported participating: N = 380)

Of much value	....	23.4
Of some value	....	29.9
Of little value	....	46.7

Principal's academy or center:
(44.2% of respondents reported participating: N = 369)

Of much value	....	21.6
Of some value	....	30.7
Of little value	....	47.7

National meetings of principals:
(68.5% of respondents reported participating: N = 571)

Of much value	....	16.6
Of some value	....	44.3
Of little value	....	39.1

Responses reflect the experiences of principals who had participated, for example, in an internship in school administration.

About 69 percent of the principals report attending national meetings of principals. Nearly 61 percent report "much or some value" in such meetings, with experience emerging as a factor in the reaction. The number of principals placing "much value" on them increased from 5.9 percent for principals with less than five years of experience to 21.2 percent for those with 15 or more. Principals reporting "much value" in attending national meetings increased by 3.2 percent from the 1978 study.

Responses to two other areas raise issues and questions for further review. Research on school effectiveness has pointed to the value of human resource development programs, both for teachers and for principals, and such programs have become mandated in many places. Thus principal academies or centers, with widely varying support levels, are now to be found in several states. However, only 44.2 percent of the survey respondents reported having participated in an academy or center, and nearly half (47.7 percent) of these say the experience was "of little value" to their success. Since academies and centers are relatively new phenomena, perhaps the latter response is more reflective of the sparsity of the experience than its usefulness. More information is needed about the types of programs offered and the relative success of their various components.

Several national reports have promoted the internship in school administration as a means of improving principal preparation—an assumption logically supported by the high ratings given to such other on-the-job experiences as teaching and serving as a principal or assistant principal. About 46 percent of the principals report participating in such programs, with 53.3 percent seeing this experience as having "much or some value" and the remaining 46.7 percent reporting "little value." Explanations for this kind of response are not evident in the data, but it appears that the profession would be wise to thoroughly study internships for those factors that distinguish good from bad before mandating this experience as an element in preparation programs.

In which of the following areas do you feel your own need for professional development is highest?

Spurred in part by the spate of national reports on education in recent years, K-8 principals have been placed in the forefront of a quest for "educational excellence." As the instructional leaders of their schools, principals have been called upon to show the way, even though the destination may not have been clarified. One of the benefits of this development has been to sharpen principals' thinking about the professional development process and to identify the professional development areas they see as being most crucial to success (see Table 34).

Just over four in ten of the respondents place "improving staff performance" high on the list of professional development needs. Other instructional leadership functions that at least 20 percent of the principals rank high include: plan-

TABLE 34—PERCEIVED NEEDS FOR PROFESSIONAL DEVELOPMENT

		Sex	
	Total	Male	Female
Improving staff performance	41.0%	40.7%	42.2%
Planning and implementation of curricular goals	27.7	29.3	20.5
Coping with political forces impacting the school	26.2	23.8	36.0
Supervision of the instructional program	25.2	27.2	16.8
Assessment/evaluation of staff	23.5	25.3	16.1
Use of effective leadership behavior	23.5	23.5	23.6
Improving student performance	22.3	23.0	19.9
Planning/organizing personal time	22.3	22.2	23.0
Assessment/evaluation of instructional program	19.3	20.5	13.7
Use of effective communications skills	19.1	18.7	21.1
Dynamics of group processes	16.8	15.7	21.1
Effective fiscal administration	10.4	9.1	15.5
Assessment/evaluation of students	4.9	5.2	3.7
Other	2.1	1.9	3.1

(Up to three responses were requested and account for percent totals which exceed 100%.)

ning and implementation of curricular goals (27.7 percent); supervision of the instructional program (25.2 percent); assessment/evaluation of staff (23.5 percent); use of effective leadership behavior (23.5 percent); and improving student performance (22.3 percent). Other areas cited by from 16 to 20 percent of the principals include assessment/evaluation of the instructional program, effective communications skills, and the dynamics of group processes.

Somewhat surprisingly, more than one in four principals (26.2 percent) placed "coping with political forces impacting the school"—an area that principals have traditionally shied away from—as the third highest professional development need in the list. Historically, elementary school principals have been somewhat reluctant to enter—or even openly acknowledge—the political framework of their school's community. That attitude is rapidly being altered, however, by trends in the nature of the principal's responsibilities—the push for school-site management, for example, and greater accountability for site-based decisions. Thus principals are more openly acknowledging the need to be prepared to deal with the myriad political forces that have an impact on the school each day. The next step is to place greater emphasis on the political aspects of school administration in principal preparation and inservice training programs.

Ranked lowest on the list of development needs are fiscal administration (10.4 percent), assessment/evaluation of students (4.9 percent), and "other" (2.1 percent). Should school-site management practices continue to spread, more principals will be given responsibility for the fiscal management of the school, and the ranking of effective fiscal administration can be expected to rise in coming studies. The low ranking (13th place) for assessment/evaluation of students, particularly when compared to the sixth place ranking for improving student performance, may best be explained by the forced-priority nature of the question. Those who ranked improving student performance higher may well have assumed this topic to be more comprehensive than assessment/evaluation of students and to actually include such assessment/evaluation practices as a key to improving student performance.

Q What are the main sources of ideas for innovations that, during the past three years, have resulted in significant changes of practice in your school?

State mandates have emerged as the chief source of innovations.

Twelve possible sources of ideas for innovations were identified in the questionnaire, and principals were asked to check up to three responses. Although the number of sources for innovation could arguably be greater than those indicated, the study attempted to force some prioritizing. Questions from previous studies forced principals to make one choice, so direct comparison of this data with that from previous studies is not possible. State mandates or initiatives clearly have become the main source of change in school practices (See Table 35). Such a choice was not even identified in the previous studies, but the high priority that individual state governors and legislatures have placed on educational reform since the 1983 publication of *A Nation At Risk* made this additional choice necessary. The 53.5 percent response is the highest that has

TABLE 35—MAIN SOURCES OF IDEAS FOR INNOVATIONS THAT, DURING THE PAST THREE YEARS, HAVE RESULTED IN SIGNIFICANT CHANGES OF PRACTICE IN YOUR SCHOOL

	Total
State mandates or initiatives	53.5%
Local workshops	41.2
Professional reading	34.0
Consultants from outside the district	29.4
Central office staff	27.7
Teachers	26.4
Other principals	17.4
College or university courses	16.2
Principals' Academy or center	12.3
State professional associations	10.6
National professional associations	9.7
Parents or other community contacts	8.7

(Up to three multiple responses were requested and account for percent totals which exceed 100%.)

been reported in NAESP's ten-year studies since this question was introduced in 1958.

Within the profession, serious reservations have been expressed regarding the effect of many of these state mandates, but the principals were not asked to make any value judgments. Meanwhile the reality of the various state initiatives was brought home with pile-driver force to the nation's K-8 principals, who instantly acquired the responsibility for seeing to it that these mandates were appropriately implemented and monitored. There incidentally appears to be a clear relationship between the pressures to implement state mandates and the importance that principals now attach to learning how to cope with the political forces that impact on the school (see Table 34).

Other sources of innovations that the respondents note as having resulted in broad changes in school practice include: local workshops (41 percent); professional reading (34 percent); consultants from outside the district (29 percent); central office staff (28 percent); and professional colleagues, including teachers (26 percent) and other principals (17 percent). College or university courses are reported to be a main source of innovation by 16.2 percent of the respondents.

SUMMARY

The 1988 study suggests that about 95 percent of the states have certification requirements for principals. Half of these arrangements require periodic recertification—80 percent of them within five years. About 94 percent of all principals possess the principal's certificate.

About 98 percent of all principals have attained at least a master's degree. The higher the educational level attained, the more likely the principal is to hold certification for administrative positions other than the principalship.

Nearly all principals report having had teaching experience at either the elementary or secondary level. They perceive preparation and experiences in the principalship and in the classroom as having the most value to success as an elementary school principal.

Improving staff performance is viewed most consistently as the area of greatest need for professional development. The principals also attach much importance to improvement in activities relating to their role as instructional leaders. Such activities include planning and implementation of curriculum, supervision of the instructional program, and strengthening student performance. Principals identify those resources closest to home—the local school district, colleges and universities, local and state principals associations—as being the most helpful sources for personal professional development (See Table 36).

TABLE 36—SOURCE OF GREATEST ASSISTANCE FOR PROFESSIONAL DEVELOPMENT

	Total	Sex	
		Male	Female
College or university	23.1%	23.8%	19.7%
Local district	33.1	31.0	41.4
State department or intermediate agency	6.4	7.4	2.6
State association of administrators	17.3	19.2	9.9
Principals' Academy or center	16.0	14.8	21.1

The principals say the main source of ideas for educational innovations during the past three years has been state mandates. As a result, principals have become much more aware of their need to learn how to deal more effectively with the various political forces that bear on schools these days.

Chapter 4

The Principal and the School

As instruments of our society, the nation's elementary and middle schools inevitably reflect our society's interests and concerns and provide clues to changing goals and priorities.

One of the most important changes on the education scene in recent years has been a reawakened recognition of the crucial nature of the early years in shaping children's later progress in school and indeed in life. A useful clue to the emergence of that understanding is found in the response to a very significant question:

 How many separately named elementary schools are under your direction?

Fewer principals are being asked to direct more than one school.

This query goes to a fundamental finding of the "Effective Schools" research during the past few years—that the key determinant of a school's effectiveness is the principal. As the late Ronald Edmunds observed (in *Social Policy*, Vol. 7, March/April 1979) "There are some bad schools with good principals but there are no good schools with bad principals." And good principals, he added, "spend most of their time out in the school—usually in the classroom."

The reference is of course to a school that has a principal's undivided time and leadership—for the full day—not to a principal who is assigned two schools, or even three, and who must spend part of the time in transit.

A decade ago the findings of the 1978 study seemed to suggest that such squandering of the principal's leadership was perfectly acceptable, and in fact there appeared to be a trend in that direction. During the last ten years, however—perhaps in response to changing community values or priorities—the trend has reversed, as Table 37 shows.

Today nearly nine out of ten principals (87.6 percent) serve just one school—5.3 percent higher than the figure for 1978 and about identical to that for 1968.

As in the past, principals who today serve two or more schools (about 12 percent of the total respondent group) are most likely to be found in rural areas (22 percent) or small towns (16 percent).

What is your school's enrollment (including kindergartners)?

Median school enrollment is 430, in a range of 24 to 1,600.

There is an astonishingly wide range, the study reveals, in the size of the nation's elementary/middle schools, with the largest having an enrollment of 1,600 and the smallest only 24 (see Table 38). Two percent of the respondents serve schools—predominantly located in rural areas or small towns—with enrollments of 100 or fewer students. On the other hand, 3 percent of the respondents indicate they are in schools that enroll 1,000 or more students, primarily in urban and suburban areas.

As in 1978, the principals who serve the largest schools tend to be those over 50 years of age (median enrollment 460) and those with the highest academic preparation (median enrollment 440). As a group, however, the respondents with 5 to 14 years of experience as a principal were in the schools with the highest mean enrollment (490).

The median enrollment of the schools served by the respondent principals is 430, the same as that reported in 1978 (see Figure 5). The mean enrollment of these schools is 472, an increase of one student over that reported in 1978. Although the percent distribution of male and female principals is nearly equal in each enrollment category, women are about twice as likely as men to head schools that enroll less than 200 students and men are more likely to head schools that enroll between 500 and 699 students. These differences are reflected primarily in schools of medium size, with male principals serving schools having a median enrollment of 440 students and female principals serving schools with a median enrollment of 400.

TABLE 37—(NUMBER OF) SEPARATELY NAMED SCHOOLS SERVED BY ELEMENTARY PRINCIPALS

Schools Served	1968 Totals	1978 Totals	1988 Totals	Community Type				Sex	
				Urban	Sub-Urban	Small Town	Rural	Male	Female
One	87.7%	82.3%	87.6%	93.8%	96.0%	83.7%	77.9%	86.2%	93.2%
Two	8.8	13.2	10.6	6.3	3.4	14.2	17.8	11.9	5.4
Three	2.0	1.9	1.3	0.0	0.6	0.8	4.3	1.5	0.7
More than Three	1.6	2.6	0.4	0.0	0.0	1.3	0.0	0.3	0.7

TABLE 38—1987 SCHOOL ENROLLMENTS (COUNTING HALF-DAY KINDERGARTNERS AS ONE)

School Enrollment	Total	Years Experience			Community Type				Sex		Age of Respondents			Degree Status	
		Less Than 5	5 to 14	15 or More	Urban	Sub-Urban	Small Town	Rural	Male	Female	40 or Less	41 to 50	Older than 50	Bachl Mast	6-Yr/ Ph.D.
Less than 100	2.0%	2.9%	1.9%	1.1%	0.5%	0.0	1.6%	6.7%	1.8%	3.0%	4.0%	0.6%	2.2%	2.6%	0.8%
100 to 199	5.7	5.9	4.4	6.3	2.7	2.0	5.1	14.0	4.8	9.0	6.7	5.2	5.2	6.3	4.5
200 to 299	12.6	15.3	13.9	9.9	10.6	4.4	18.0	16.9	12.7	12.7	16.5	13.3	8.9	14.1	9.8
300 to 399	20.8	24.1	18.5	19.9	17.6	19.2	22.3	23.6	20.7	20.5	21.0	21.2	20.4	19.7	22.4
400 to 499	20.9	21.8	19.3	22.8	19.1	28.6	22.7	12.4	20.7	22.3	19.6	21.2	21.9	20.9	21.5
500 to 699	22.7	16.5	24.3	26.1	25.5	31.5	16.8	17.4	24.4	16.3	19.2	24.5	23.7	21.4	25.6
700 to 999	11.9	10.6	13.9	11.0	17.0	10.8	12.1	7.9	11.6	13.3	10.7	11.2	13.3	11.7	12.6
1,000 or more	3.2	2.9	3.8	2.9	6.9	3.4	1.6	1.1	3.3	3.0	2.2	2.7	4.4	3.3	2.8
Median	430	400	440	450	480	480	400	349	440	400	400	430	460	430	440
Mean	472														
Range—Low	24														
High	1600														

FIGURE 5—MEDIAN ENROLLMENT IN SCHOOLS SINCE 1928

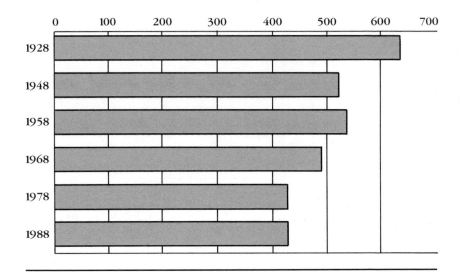

The data seem to indicate that the enrollment declines in K-8 school have leveled off. However, demographic studies project sharp enrollment increases in some parts of the country during the next decade, while in other areas enrollments will continue decline.

 What is your school district's approximate enrollment?

School district enrollments vary all over the landscape.

The responses to this question underscore the wide discrepancy in size of school districts in the United States (see Table 39). Two percent of the respondents work in districts enrolling fewer than 300 students, approximately 38 percent in districts with 300 to 2,499 students, 34 percent in districts with 2,500 to 9,999 students, 15 percent in districts enrolling 10,000 to 24,999 students, and 11 percent in districts larger than 25,000 students.

Although male and female principals are distributed fairly evenly across the various size districts, those with enrollments of 300 to 2,499 students are nearly twice as likely

TABLE 39—APPROXIMATE ENROLLMENT OF SCHOOL DISTRICT SERVED BY RESPONDENTS
(Count half-day kindergarten pupils as one pupil each)

| District Enrollment | Total | Sex | |
		Male	Female
Less than 300	2.0%	2.0%	2.0%
300 to 2,499	37.8	41.4	22.5
2,500 to 9,999	34.4	33.0	39.7
10,000 to 24,999 ..	14.6	14.3	15.9
25,000 or more ...	11.2	9.2	19.9

to have male principals in the elementary and middle schools. On the other hand, districts enrolling more than 25,000 students are twice as likely to have female principals.

How would you characterize the community which your school serves?

Most survey respondents work in small towns and rural areas.

In previous studies in this ten-year series, the respondents were given three choices in responding to this question: urban, suburban, and rural. The current study provides five choices: large urban, medium urban, suburban, small town, and rural. No attempt was made to provide specific definitions for each category.

It develops that just over half of the respondents (see Table 40) serve either small towns (31 percent) or rural communities (21.5 percent). About 7 percent are in large urban communities, another 16 percent in medium urban communities, and the remaining 24.7 percent in suburban communities.

Slight differences in the type of community served and the level of academic preparation of principals were noted in the responses to this question. About 55 percent of the principals who had a sixth year of preparation or the doctorate were found in suburban, medium urban, and large urban areas, while small towns and rural communities employed this same percent (55) of principals with the bachelor's or master's degree.

TABLE 40—TYPES OF COMMUNITIES SERVED BY PRINCIPALS

Community Type	Total	Sex		Degree Held	
		Male	Female	Bach/Mast	6-Yr/ Ph.D.
Large Urban	6.9%	5.0%	14.6%	6.7%	6.6%
Medium Urban	16.0	16.1	15.9	14.5	20.1
Suburban	24.7	24.7	23.8	23.6	27.9
Small Town	31.0	32.7	23.8	33.3	24.6
Rural	21.5	21.5	22.0	21.9	20.9

Regarding gender differences, while both males and females are well represented in the principalship within each type of community, large urban areas are more likely to employ females as principals and small towns to employ males. Small towns evidently have been less successful than urban areas in the application of affirmative action procedures to assure equity.

What is the approximate composition of the pupil enrollment of your school?

Indications are that the future will bring more and more at-risk students.

Demographic studies in recent years have pointed to the emergence of dramatic changes in the composition of student enrollments. Our schools will be confronted by increasing numbers of at-risk students—students the schools have traditionally served least well.

Urban areas (see Table 41) already are reflecting some of the kinds of changes that may be anticipated during the coming years; the data indicate, for example, that Caucasians currently make up only about 55 percent of K-8 enrollments in the cities. Meanwhile Harold Hodgkinson has reported (in the January 1986 *Principal*, p. 11) that today "each of the nation's 24 largest city school systems has a minority majority" and that the birth and immigration rates among Hispanic, black, and Asian/Pacific Islanders make them the nation's most rapidly growing populations. Thus the current distribution of enrollments doubtless will be markedly different by the time of the next NAESP study ten years hence, a demographic shift that is likely to give rise to

TABLE 41—APPROXIMATE MEAN DISTRIBUTION OF THE COMPOSITION OF STUDENT ENROLLMENT (PERCENT) BY COMMUNITY TYPE

	Total	Urban	Sub-Urban	Small Town	Rural
Hispanic	7	13	6	6	5
Native American	1	1	1	2	2
Asian/Pacific Islander	2	3	3	1	0
Black	10	24	5	8	6
White	76	55	82	81	84
Other	4	4	3	2	3

a number of new issues to confront K-8 principals over the next decade.

Is your school accredited by any agency other than the state?

Accreditation beyond the state level is rising.

Regional accreditation for secondary schools has been a common practice since the early 1900s, but such accreditation was not available at the K-8 level until the Southern Association of Colleges and Schools began to accredit elementary schools in December 1960. The North Central Association Commission on Schools followed suit during the 1974-75 school year, and the Middle States Association joined the movement in 1979. The Northwest and Western Associations were the next to take up elementary school accreditation, and when the New England Association of Schools went along in 1985, regional accreditation became available to all elementary schools throughout the United States. Similar accreditation programs for private schools, operated by such agencies as the Independent Schools Association of the Central States and the National Catholic Educational Association, have also become available during this period.

Today about one in five elementary schools across the country (see Table 42) have taken up some type of accreditation other than that of the state. The two largest regional accrediting associations, the North Central Associa-

TABLE 42—SCHOOLS ACCREDITED BY AN AGENCY OTHER THAN THE STATE

	Total
Is your school accredited by an agency other than the state?	
Yes	20.9%
No	78.9
First accredited	
Before 1970	22.2
1970-1979	42.7
1980 or later	35.0
Accredited by	
Southern Assn of Colleges & Schools	54.4
North Central Association	32.0
Middle States Association	1.2
No agency specified	12.4

tion and the Southern Association, have accredited elementary schools the longest and thus provide the best measure of the extent of the movement. Of the schools that the survey respondents report as being accredited by an agency other than the state, the Southern Association Commission on Elementary Schools accounts for more than half (54.4 percent) and the North Central Association Commission on Schools about a third (32 percent). No specific accrediting agency was identified by 12.4 percent of these respondents, while another 1.2 percent indicated that their school was accredited by the Middle States Association.

Of the accredited schools, the Southern Association Commission on Schools has at least 30 percent higher representation from urban and rural areas than does the North Central Association Commission on Schools, and a 20 percent higher representation from suburban areas. Representation from small towns is nearly equal in both accrediting commissions. The differences seem more likely to be a reflection of the policies of the two regional accrediting agencies (along with the number of years each has been accrediting elementary schools) than of varying interests among principals within the two regions. The Southern Association has a long history of incentives that encourage system-wide accreditation of individual schools within large urban districts; the North Central Association has only recently begun to move in that direction.

At any rate, there would appear to be the beginnings of a trend toward increased numbers of elementary schools becoming accredited by agencies other than the state.

During the current school year, are any of the pupils in your school being bused to achieve or maintain racial balance?

School busing is clearly on the decline.

This and the following question were repeated from the 1978 study, but the 1988 responses were too sparse to permit a valid generalization and thus tables focused on them have not been included in this report. However, approximately 10 percent of the respondents (a decline of 1.2 percent from the total reported in 1978) indicate that pupils in their school are indeed being bused to achieve or maintain racial balance. Such busing was reported by 30 percent of the urban respondents and by 5.5 percent or less of the respondents from other community types.

During the current school year, are any of the pupils in your school district being bused to achieve or maintain racial balance?

Nearly 18 percent of the respondents report that their school districts are involved in busing programs to achieve or maintain racial balance. More than half of the urban districts have such programs, and nearly 11 percent of the suburban districts.

Do you have an assistant principal assigned to your school?

The assistant principalship is becoming a far more common position.

The number of assistant principals is reported to have increased by nearly 13 percent during the past ten years, and today such positions are to be found in nearly one-third of the nation's K-8 schools (see Table 43). Assistant principals are on the staff of three-fourths of the schools that enroll more than 600 pupils, and more than one-third of those that enroll 400 to 600. Nearly two-thirds of these assistant principals serve on a full-time basis, with one in five serving part time. Nearly 9 percent of the schools have *two* full-time assistants, more than double the number reported in 1978.

TABLE 43—ASSIGNMENT OF ASSISTANT PRINCIPALS

	Total
Do you have an assistant principal assigned to your school?	
Yes	32.4%
No	67.6
If Yes, How many?	
Fulltime— One	63.2
Two	8.6
More than Two	4.1
Part-time—One	21.1
Two	0.4
More than Two	0.0
What allocation formula used?	
Based on school enrollment	46.2
Assigned to all elementary and/or intermediate levels	25.3
Based on number of staff members	7.2
Assigned to work with specific programs	6.2
Other	15.1
What major responsibilities?	
Duties as assigned	16.3
Supervision/evaluation of teachers	14.4
Supervision/evaluation of nonteaching staff	8.1
Curriculum development	8.1
Discipline/student management	19.5
Student evaluation/placement	8.8
Parent/community contacts	11.0
Facilities management	8.7
Budget administration	2.4
Other	2.6

The principals with assistant principals were asked to identify the kind of allocation system that was used in assigning an assistant to their school. The most frequent response was that assignments were based on school enrollment (46 percent). An additional 25 percent said it was simply a matter of *all* elementary and intermediate schools in the district being assigned an assistant. About 7 percent said such assignments were based on the number of staff members, and 6 percent said the assistant was assigned to work with specific programs. Some type of "other" allocation was reported by 15 percent of the respondents.

The principals who had assistants assigned to their building were also asked to identify the assistant principals' major responsibilities. Discipline and student management were reported by about 20 percent of the respondents, with 16 percent indicating "duties as assigned," 14 percent saying supervision and evaluation of teachers, and 11 percent parent and community contacts. Between 8 and 9 percent of assistant principals focus chiefly on student evaluation and placement, facilities management, curriculum development, and supervision and evaluation of the nonteaching staff, while 2.5 percent are given budget administration responsibilities.

No outstanding differences were noted between genders as to which principals were assigned an assistant principal or in the manner in which the assistant was asked to serve.

How many of the following professional staff are currently assigned to your school?

More K-8 staffs are including specialists like librarians and counselors.

The typical elementary school staff today includes 21 full-time classroom teachers (see Table 44). The median number is 19, one more than the number reported in the 1968 and 1978 studies. The mean number of teachers assigned to a school increases with pupil enrollment; for example, the difference between schools with an enrollment of less than 400 and those enrolling between 400 and 600 students is eight teachers, a rise that could be expected with an additional section or group of students at each grade level.

Because a different response distribution was used in the current study, direct comparisons with the findings from previous studies are not possible. However, since enrollments reported by schools in the current study have remained almost identical to those reported ten years ago, it can be assumed that the distribution of teachers has not been radically modified, though it is also possible that a number of current state reform efforts aimed at reducing class size in the primary grades (e.g., Indiana's "Prime Time") are beginning to affect the number of teachers assigned to elementary schools.

For the first time in this series of studies, the 1988 version sought to get a handle on the incidence of part-time teachers used in K-8 schools. While nearly seven of ten principals (69.2 percent) say they have no part-time classroom teachers at all, job-sharing programs have been initiated in a number of school districts and appear to be gaining support across the country.

TABLE 44—NUMBER OF CLASSROOM TEACHERS ASSIGNED TO ELEMENTARY SCHOOLS

Classroom Teachers	Total	Size of School		
		Less than 400	400-600	More than 600
Full-time:				
10 or less	11.0%	25.7%	0.6%	1.1%
11-15	22.4	47.8	7.2	1.1
16-20	23.5	19.8	41.0	3.3
21-25	16.9	3.9	31.1	18.5
More than 25	26.2	2.7	20.1	76.0
Part-time				
None	69.2	70.5	66.0	71.6
1	12.4	11.3	14.3	11.5
2	7.7	8.0	7.8	7.1
3-5	7.3	6.9	9.5	4.9
More than 5	3.3	3.3	2.4	4.8
Mean	21	14	22	35
Median	19			

(Mean figures refer to average number of full-time classroom teachers, excluding special area teachers.)

The study shows that today a mean of four and a median of three full-time special-area teachers are assigned to each elementary school (see Table 45), and when schools reporting no special area teachers are eliminated, both the mean and median figures increase by one. The number of special-area teachers per school varies considerably; as with classroom teachers, the number is directly related to the size of the school. Part-time special-area teachers are to be found in more than half (53 percent) of today's K-8 schools.

These staffs also include a number of other professionals (see Table 46). Full-time librarian/media specialists are the most common, with nearly 60 percent of the principals reporting one or more such persons in their school. This

TABLE 45—NUMBER OF SPECIAL AREA TEACHERS IN ELEMENTARY SCHOOLS

		Size of School		
Special area teachers	Total	Less than 400	400-600	More than 600
Full-time				
None	17.4%	26.0%	13.3%	8.3%
One	12.0	20.7	7.1	3.9
Two	15.8	18.9	16.0	10.0
Three	13.2	10.8	17.3	11.1
Four	10.0	10.2	10.9	8.3
5-9	22.9	11.4	25.6	40.6
10 or more	8.5	2.1	9.6	17.8
Part-time				
None	47.0	39.2	47.3	61.1
One	13.8	14.7	13.4	12.8
Two	11.5	9.3	14.4	11.1
Three or four	14.7	18.6	13.7	8.9
Five or more	12.8	18.3	10.9	6.3
Mean	4	2	4	6
Median	3			

(Mean figures refer only to full-time special area teachers.)

TABLE 46—NUMBER OF OTHER PROFESSIONAL STAFF MEMBERS IN ELEMENTARY SCHOOLS

Position	None	One	More than One
Full-time Nurse	79.4%	19.2%	1.4%
Part-time Nurse	43.5	54.6	1.9
Full-time Counselor	60.7	28.8	10.5
Part-time Counselor	64.8	33.1	2.1
Full-time Librarian/Media Specialist	40.6	57.0	2.4
Part-time Librarian/Media Specialist	66.1	32.2	1.6
Full-time Other Professionals	85.4	7.4	7.2
Part-time Other Professionals	75.8	13.8	10.4

represents a increase of 12.4 percent since 1978 and continues a steady growth in full-time elementary school library/media specialists that was first noted in the 1958 study. Another 34 percent of the principals report having one or more part-time library/media specialists.

Also becoming more available in K-8 schools are counseling services, with just over 39 percent of the principals saying that their school's staff includes at least one full-time counselor (an increase of 23.4 percent in the past decade); and another 35.2 percent saying they have one or more counselors on a part-time basis (an increase of 8.3 percent). At the same time, however, more than half of the principals say they have no full-time counselors (or nurses) at all.

About one in five principals (20.6 percent) say their staff includes one or more full-time nurses, and another 56.5 percent have one or more part-time nurses.

One or more "other" full-time professional staff members were reported by 14.6 percent of the respondents, and another 24.2 percent on a part-time basis. Both of these figures are lower than those reported in previous studies, most likely because of the inclusion of nurses in the previous figures. Although these "other" professional staff members were not identified by title, it is probable that the majority consist of such pupil service providers as speech clinicians, audiologists, psychologists, social workers, and special curriculum/program consultants, many of whose assignments are itinerant by nature.

How many of the following support staff are assigned to your school?

Management of personnel has become a bigger element of the principal's job.

Previous ten-year studies have included a support-staff question focused simply on the provision of teacher aides and secretarial/clerical staff. For this study the question was expanded to include additional types of support staff positions and thus provide more information about the extent to which K-8 principals are involved in the management of noninstructional personnel.

Nearly 54 percent of the principals (see Table 47) report the availability of one full-time secretary or clerical assistant. An additional 26.9 percent say they have two such full-time persons, and another 12 percent report three or more. The total number of schools with at least one full-time secretary or clerical assistant (92.8 percent) represents a gain of nearly 5 percent since 1978. An additional 20.2 percent of the respondents reported one or more part-time secretaries or clerical assistants.

Full-time teacher aides are present in 74.6 percent of the K-8 schools today, and the mean number of such aides is three. (If the schools reporting no aides are excluded from the mean calculation, this figure increases to four.) Additionally, nearly 29 percent more schools have one or more part-time teacher aides. These figures represent an increase in full-time aides of just over 7 percent during the past ten years, and a decrease of about 6 percent in part-time aides.

Regarding other support staff positions, although some districts have turned to employing health aids rather than school nurses (as a cost-saving measure), the study shows that this practice is not widespread: Only 6.8 percent of the principals say they have one or more full-time health aides in their school, with another 9.4 percent reporting one or more on a part-time basis.

More than 95 percent of the principals say their support staff includes one or more full-time custodians. More than half of these principals (52 percent) say they have either

TABLE 47—NUMBER OF SUPPORT STAFF ASSIGNED TO ELEMENTARY SCHOOLS

Position	None	One	More Than One	Two	More Than Two	Three	More Than Three	Four	Five or More	Five to Nine	Ten or More
Full-Time Teacher Aides	25.4%	16.0%		13.4%		14.9%		7.2%		12.1%	11.0%
Part-Time Teacher Aides	61.3	16.1		6.1		3.6		3.0		6.4	3.4
Full-Time Secretary/Clerical	7.1	53.9		26.9		6.7	5.3				
Part-Time Secretary/Clerical	79.8	18.0	2.2								
Full-Time Health Aide	93.2	6.1	0.7								
Part-Time Health Aide	90.6	8.3	1.1								
Full-Time Custodian	4.4	22.0		30.2		21.8		7.8	13.7		
Part-Time Custodian	66.3	23.7		5.9	4.0						
Full-Time Cafeteria Workers	30.2	8.9		13.0		11.8		11.4	24.7		
Part-Time Cafeteria Workers	46.3	17.2		14.6		6.8		6.0	8.7		
Full-Time Other Support Personnel	85.4	7.4	7.2								
Part-Time Other Support Personnel	75.8	13.8	10.4								

two (30.2 percent) or three (21.8 percent) full-time custodians, with 34 percent reporting one or more on a part-time basis.

Full-time cafeteria workers are reported by about 70 percent of the principals who responded to this question. Approximately one-third of this group (35.4 percent) have four or more such workers, and another 24.4 percent have either two or three. In addition, about 17 percent of the principals say they also have one part-time cafeteria worker and another 36 percent report two or more part-timers.

About 15 percent of the respondents reported that their support staff includes one or more full-time persons in an "other" capacity (not identified) and another 24 percent have one or more part-time persons doing "other" work.

What is the male to female composition of your teaching staff?

Women continue to be dominant on the staffs of K-8 schools.

Teaching staffs in K-8 schools continue to be predominantly female, with four of every five teachers being a woman (see Table 48). The proportion of schools reporting no men at all on the staff increased from 1 percent in 1978 to 7.3 percent today. Nearly 40 percent of the schools report that 90 percent or more of their faculty members are women, while less than 1 percent of the schools report 70 percent or more of their faculty to be men.

The proportions of men and women reported in 1988 do not differ significantly from those in previous studies.

What is the approximate ethnic composition of your teaching staff?

About 89 percent of school staffs are Caucasian.

Whatever the demographic trends in the ethnicity of American students, K-8 teaching staffs (see Table 49) remain predominantly (89 percent) Caucasian. The study indicates that 7 percent are black, three percent Hispanic, and another 1 percent native American. The number of Asian/Pacific Islanders or members of other nonwhite ethnic groups was too small to figure in the compilation.

The greatest mix of ethnic groups is found in urban communities, where blacks constitute 17 percent of teach-

TABLE 48—MALE-FEMALE RATIO IN ELEMENTARY TEACHING STAFF

Percent	Sex	
	Male	Female
None	7.3	0.2
Less than 10	22.2	0.2
10-19	25.8	0.1
20-29	16.6	0.4
30-39	7.9	0.6
40-49	9.0	3.0
50-59	8.3	10.2
60-69	2.0	9.4
70-79	0.4	13.1
80-89	0.1	23.3
90-99	0.1	32.1
100	0.2	7.3

TABLE 49—APPROXIMATE ETHNIC MEAN COMPOSITION OF ELEMENTARY
TEACHING STAFF

			Community Type		
	Total Mean	Urban	Sub-Urban	Small Town	Rural
Hispanic	3%	4%	2%	2%	3%
Native American	1	0	1	1	1
Asian/Pacific Islander	0	1	0	0	0
Black	7	17	3	5	4
White	89	77	94	92	92
Other Non-white	0	1	0	0	0

ing staffs, Hispanics 4 percent, native Americans 1 percent, other nonwhites 1 percent, and whites 77 percent. In suburban, small town, and rural communities, the teaching staffs are at least 92 percent Caucasian.

Do you have a student council in your school?

Slightly more than half (50.8 percent) of the principals in the study report having a student council in their school, and another 11.2 percent say they are discussing the idea (see Table 50). With a growing public concern for helping students develop leadership skills, and with NAESP having launched the American Student Council Association, the number of student councils can be expected to have increased rather substantially by the time of the next ten-year study.

TABLE 50—PRESENCE OF A STUDENT COUNCIL IN ELEMENTARY SCHOOLS

	Total
Do you have a student council in your school?	
Yes	50.8%
No, but being discussed or planned	11.2
No	38.0

How would you describe the attitude of parents toward your school and its program?

School/parent relationships are reported to be very good.

Numerous scholars have written in recent years about the close connection between children's success in school and the attitude of parents toward the school and their involvement in the school's work. As the study shows, today's K-8 schools are doing a good job in fostering this kind of school-parent cooperation (see Figure 6). Just over 46 percent of the principals say their students' parents are "highly supportive and involved" and an additional 52.5 percent say the parents are "supportive" but have "little involvement." Less than 3 percent of the respondents in any type of community reported parents to be "neither supportive nor involved."

With the notable exception of responses from suburban principals, the "highly supportive and involved" responses ranged between 37 and 44 percent, with "supportive but little involvement" responses ranging from 55 to 60 percent. In suburban communities, nearly 60 percent of the principals say parents are "highly supportive and involved" and another 39.5 percent indicate "supportive but little involvement." The "highly supportive and involved" finding

FIGURE 6—PARENTS' ATTITUDES TOWARD YOUR SCHOOL AND PROGRAM

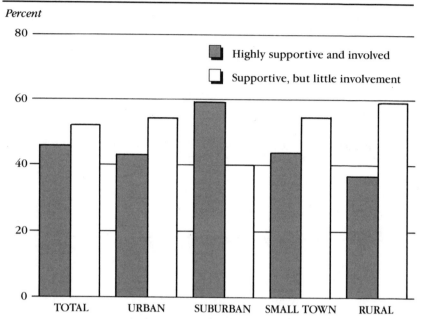

Percent

☐ Highly supportive and involved

☐ Supportive, but little involvement

TOTAL   URBAN   SUBURBAN   SMALL TOWN   RURAL

Less than 3% of the respondents in any of these categories responded "Neither supportive nor involved."

seems especially remarkable, given the rapidly increasing number of homes in which no parent is at home during the day.

Q **How would you characterize the extent to which parent volunteers are involved in your school's educational program?**

Volunteers are present every day in almost half of K-8 schools.

A remarkably high number of the principals—about 40 percent—report that "parents work in the school on a daily basis" (see Table 51). More than half (52.1 percent) of the women and just over one-third of the men (36.4 percent) report such intensive volunteer activity in their schools. Because demographic studies suggest that many if not most parents are unavailable to help in the schools during the

TABLE 51—EXTENT OF PARENT VOLUNTEERS IN THE EDUCATIONAL PROGRAM

| | | Community Type | | | | Sex | |
	Total	Urban	Sub-Urban	Small Town	Rural	Male	Female
Parents working in school on a daily basis	39.6%	42.8%	53.2%	31.8%	32.2%	36.4%	52.1%
Involvement is limited to special projects	48.2	40.6	36.0	58.8	54.8	50.3	40.0
Little or no involvement by parent volunteers	12.2	16.6	10.8	9.4	13.0	13.3	7.9

school day, the assumption is that the actual *number* of parents who do such volunteer work within any individual school may be relatively small.

Nearly half (48.2 percent) of the respondents say parent involvement is "limited to special projects." Participation of this focused nature has long marked the relationship between parents and K-8 schools, is widely encouraged by teachers and principals, and has helped to assure that adequate assistance and supervision is available to students during special activities and events. However, more than 12 percent of the principals (13.3 percent of the males and 7.9 percent of the females) indicate that there is "little to no involvement by parent volunteers."

Does your school have a parents' advisory council that is sometimes involved with curriculum issues?

Parent advisory councils are now almost standard.

It would appear that nearly 60 percent of the nation's K-8 schools have a parent advisory council that at least on occasion gets involved with curriculum issues (see Table 52). Such councils are reported by nearly two-thirds of urban and suburban principals and about half of the small town and rural principals. A slightly higher percentage of female principals (61.2) than male (55.4) report having such councils.

What is the approximate percent of the student body in your school that is from single-parent and latchkey homes?

The "latchkey" child situation is not just a "city" problem.

A major challenge to K-8 schools that was not recognized as an area of concern in the 1978 study is the number of children who reside in single-parent homes or in homes in which both parents work—leaving youngsters on their own after classes are over until a parent comes home from work: the so-called latchkey children.

The principals report that today about 22 percent of their students come from single-parent families and 15 percent are in a latchkey situation (see Table 53). Such figures are cause for concern, but even more distressing is the

TABLE 52—PARENTS' ADVISORY COUNCIL SOMETIMES INVOLVED WITH CURRICULUM ISSUES

	Total	Urban	Community Type		Rural	Sex	
			Sub-Urban	Small Town		Male	Female
Yes	56.7%	65.4%	60.3%	48.4%	55.1%	55.4%	61.2%
No	43.3	34.6	39.7	51.6	44.9	44.6	38.8

TABLE 53—APPROXIMATE PERCENT OF SINGLE PARENT AND LATCHKEY CHILDREN IN URBAN, SUBURBAN, SMALL TOWN AND RURAL COMMUNITIES

SINGLE PARENT

Percent	Totals	Urban	Community Type		Rural
			Sub-Urban	Small Town	
Less than 20	13.1	5.8	16.2	12.1	18.6
20-29...........................	13.3	9.0	13.8	16.9	12.4
30-39...........................	18.0	15.9	23.2	18.4	14.6
40-49...........................	10.4	14.3	9.4	10.6	7.3
50 or more	13.2	28.1	7.4	10.6	8.0
Don't know/No response	32.0	27.0	30.0	31.4	39.1

LATCHKEY

Percent	Totals	Urban	Community Type		Rural
			Sub-Urban	Small Town	
Less than 20	16.8	12.7	17.2	18.7	18.5
20-29...........................	9.0	7.4	10.3	6.6	12.9
30-39...........................	7.2	7.4	6.9	9.0	5.1
40-49...........................	5.9	7.9	5.4	6.6	3.4
50 or more	11.3	19.0	10.3	8.6	7.9
Don't know/No response	49.8	45.5	49.9	50.5	52.2

proportion of respondents who either say they "don't know" the extent of such problems in their schools or who failed to respond (a likely indication that they don't know, either). One in three principals (32.4 percent) was unsure of the number of students who lived in single-parent homes, and slightly more than half (50.2 percent) didn't know the number of latchkey children in their schools.

The conventional notion is that the problems associated with single-parent homes and latchkey children are essentially "city" matters. The 1988 study confirms that these problems are indeed most common in urban areas, but the data also show that suburbia and small towns and rural communities are by no means immune.

 How would you describe your relationships with each of the parties listed below?

K-8 principals enjoy very good relationships.

The "parties" cited in the question consisted of the school board, the superintendent, other central office staff, teachers, students, parents, and the community as a whole. Nine out of ten principals perceive their relationships with each of these groups as being either "excellent" or "good" (see Table 54). Relationships with students drew the most frequent "excellent" rating (63.5 percent), and relationships with the school board the least frequent (42.8 percent). The lowest ratings were given to relationships with the two parties they see least often and who are farthest removed from the school's daily operations—the school board (1.6 percent "poor" and 5.7 percent "fair") and the superintendent (1.1 percent "poor" and 6.8 percent "fair"). No "poor" ratings were reported with students or parents, and negligible "poor" ratings were reported with teachers and community (.1 percent each) and other central office staff (.2 percent).

SUMMARY

About 88 percent of the principals in the 1988 study have responsibility for a single school and for an average of 472 students. About 53 percent serve rural and small town communities. And of the principals with education beyond the master's degree, 55 percent are found in suburban or urban areas.

The demographic developments under way in the United States are most closely reflected in what is happening in urban schools, where Caucasian students make up only about 55 percent of overall enrollments, as contrasted with more than 80 percent in the suburbs, small towns, and rural areas. The principals report about a 10 percent decline in the busing of students for purposes of desegregation since

TABLE 54—PRINCIPALS' PERCEPTION OF THEIR RELATIONSHIPS WITH EACH OF THE PARTIES LISTED BELOW

	Total
School Board:	
Excellent	43.0%
Good	49.7
Fair	5.7
Poor	1.6
Superintendent:	
Excellent	55.9%
Good	36.0
Fair	6.9
Poor	1.1
Other Central Office Staff:	
Excellent	54.0%
Good	41.8
Fair	4.0
Poor	0.2
Teachers:	
Excellent	54.5%
Good	43.6
Fair	1.8
Poor	0.1
Students:	
Excellent	63.6%
Good	35.7
Fair	0.7
Poor	0.0
Parents:	
Excellent	46.6%
Good	50.4
Fair	2.9
Poor	0.0
Community:	
Excellent	46.3%
Good	50.3
Fair	3.3
Poor	0.1

1978, but such programs nevertheless continue in over 17 percent of the school districts.

The average school staff reported in the study consists of 21 full-time classroom teachers, four full-time special area teachers, three teacher aides, and at least one secretary/ clerical assistant. Although members of minorities are reported to make up about 11 percent of overall elementary-middle school staffs, in the cities the proportion is 23 percent. Women make up 80 percent of the faculty of K-8 schools, but men occupy 80 percent of the principalships.

With arrangements for elementary school accreditation now available across the country, nearly 20 percent of the schools represented in the study are being accredited by some agency other than the state. These schools are found almost exclusively in the regions of the Southern and North Central associations.

Just over half of the schools have a student council, and six out of ten have a parent advisory council that gets involved with curriculum matters. About 40 percent of the principals report that parent volunteers work in their schools on a daily basis, while another 48 percent say parent volunteers serve the school on a special projects basis. More than 98 percent of the principals describe parental attitudes toward their school and its programs as either highly supportive and involved or supportive but with little involvement.

Overall, the principals of today's elementary and middle schools feel good about their school and enjoy the people they work with. Their relationships seem to be best with the people they deal with most often (i.e. students, teachers, and parents), and less close but still either "good" or "excellent" with people they see only occasionally (i.e., members of school boards and superintendents).

Chapter 5

Contracts and Conditions of Employment

C onditions of the workplace are of course critical factors in determining how much satisfaction principals derive from their job.

Contractual arrangements, terms of employment, salary and fringe benefits, the length and content of a typical work day, the functions and responsibilities that command the most time—such matters invariably have a major bearing on morale and job satisfaction. Hence this question:

 Do you have a personal contract with your school district? If yes, what is the term of your contract?

Most K-8 principals have personal service contracts.

For a leader who must be prepared to make some tough decisions, the sense of stability and security that goes with a personal contract with the school district is of crucial importance. Further, the offering of a contract, particularly a multiyear contract, is also a measure of confidence.

Perhaps one reason why the leadership in K-8 education is so strong is the fact that 87.5 percent of all principals are covered by such a contract (see Table 55). About 40 percent of these contracts extend over one year, with an additional 30 percent being of a continuing nature—that is, they remain in effect unless the principal is notified of termination. Multi-year contracts are reported by 27 percent of the respondents, with 19 percent holding contracts for two years and the remaining 7 percent for three. Multiyear contracts are least prevalent (12.6 percent) in urban communities. About one in four principals in urban, small town, and rural communities report their contract is for two or three years.

 Do you have a written agreement with your school district which specifies your salary, benefits, and working conditions?

Employment conditions today are being spelled out.

More than 80 percent of all principals have a contract with the school district that specifies salary, benefits, and working conditions (see Table 56). Just ten years ago this figure was only 65 percent. In the current study a distinction is made between a master agreement for all principals (53.1 percent of the total) and a contract specifically tailored to an individual principal and school (28.3 percent)—the first time the ten-year study has done so.

TABLE 55—WRITTEN CONTRACTS FOR PRINCIPALS

	Total 1988
Is a written contract provided?	
Yes	87.5%
No	12.5
If yes, what is the term of your contract?	
1 Year	40.2%
2 Years	18.6
3 Years	8.5
Continuing	30.4
Other	2.3

TABLE 56—WRITTEN AGREEMENTS WHICH SPECIFY SALARY, BENEFITS, AND WORKING CONDITIONS

1978	Totals	1988	Totals
Yes	65.2%	Yes, master agreement for all principals	53.1%
		Yes, although each principal's contract may be different	28.3
No	34.8	No	18.5

While there has been a substantial improvement in the proportion of K-8 principals covered by a written contract, the fact remains that about 18.5 percent still lack that protection.

What is your 1986-87 salary as a principal?

The mean annual salary of K-8 principals is almost $40,000.

The mean* salary paid K-8 principals in 1987 was $39,988 (see Table 57). About 26 percent of all principals report earning less than $35,000 annually, while the earnings of 11 percent of all principals exceed $50,000.

A comparison of mean salaries (see Table 58) reveals some interesting data. The reported salary of men is $40,312, while that for women is $38,677. Traditionally, principal salaries have been at least partially based on such factors as years of experience, size of school, academic preparation levels, and type of community (with average suburban salaries the highest). That tradition still prevails.

The average principal salary increased from $6,237 in 1958 to $39,988 in 1987. During this time span, however, rises in the cost of living have consumed 75 percent of the value of the dollar; the 1958 dollar value would be only $.25 today (see Table 59). Still, salary gains have kept ahead of inflation, so that the actual purchasing power (or "real dollars") has increased by $3,760 (60 percent) over the past 30 years. The past decade, however, has been a somewhat different story. Despite a mean salary increase of $18,488 since 1978, the "real gain" (in 1958 dollars) during this time span has been a modest $537.

Does your district have merit or incentive pay for principals?

17 percent of K-8 principals have merit pay arrangements.

Among the items that appeared on the national agenda following the Department of Education's publication of *A Nation At Risk* has been the concept of rewarding teachers

---

* The data in this study are the first to report mean rather than median salaries, so some of the long-term comparisons found in previous reports are not included in this report.

TABLE 57—COMPARISON OF PRINCIPAL SALARIES IN 1987

| Salary Range | Total | Size of School | | | Community Type | | | |
		Less than 400	400-600	More than 600	Urban	Sub-Urban	Small Town	Rural
Less than $35,000	26.3%	42.1%	17.9%	11.5%	12.6%	6.6%	38.3%	47.4%
$35,000—$39,999	24.7	27.0	26.6	17.5	19.2	12.6	34.3	30.4
$40,000—$44,999	21.2	14.8	23.8	28.4	29.1	24.2	16.9	15.2
$45,000—$49,999	16.6	9.7	20.0	23.5	24.7	27.8	9.3	5.3
$50,000 or more	11.3	6.4	11.7	19.1	14.3	28.8	1.2	1.8
Mean	$39,988							

TABLE 58—COMPARISON OF MEAN PRINCIPAL SALARIES IN 1987

Comparison Group	Mean Salary
Urban	$42,661
Suburban	45,164
Small Town	36,946
Rural	35,311
Male	40,312
Female	38,677
Enrollment less than 400	36,932
400-600 enrollment	41,317
More than 600 enrollment	43,230
Less than 5 years experience	36,706
5-14 years experience	39,720
15 or more years experience	42,678
Bachelor's/Master's Degree	42,984
6-Yr/Ph.D. Degree	43,314
Total Mean	39,988

TABLE 59—PRINCIPAL SALARIES ADJUSTED TO 1958 DOLLAR

Years	1958 Dollar Value	Actual Mean Salary	Salaries Adj. to 1958 Dollar
1958	1.00	$6237	$6237
1968	.83	9700	8051
1978	.44	21,500	9460
1987	.25	39,988	9997

and principals for work that exceeds the school district's normal expectations. Defining and measuring "normal" is not easy, and the instinct of school district managers is to rely on scores in student achievement tests as a basic measure of meritorious service.

Currently about 17 percent of the elementary and middle school principals are involved in a merit or incentive pay program (see Table 60), with such programs being most commonly found in suburban (22.9 percent) and urban

TABLE 60—DISTRICT MERIT OR INCENTIVE PAY FOR PRINCIPALS

| | Total | Urban | Community Type | | | Sex | |
			Sub-Urban	Small Town	Rural	Male	Female
Yes	17.0%	20.7%	22.9%	14.7%	10.7%	17.4%	15.7%
No	83.0	79.3	77.1	85.3	89.3	82.6	84.3

If yes, is any portion based on your students' achievement?

Yes	23.7	36.8	21.4	13.9	21.1	23.6	24.0
No	76.3	63.2	78.6	86.1	78.9	76.4	76.0

communities (20.7 percent). Men (17.4 percent) seem slightly more likely to be involved in such incentive pay programs than are women (15.7 percent).

Of the 17 percent of respondents covered by merit or incentive pay programs, the salary of about one in four (23.7 percent) is at least in part based on how well the school's students perform in the classroom. This kind of arrangement, with salary levels being tied to student achievement levels, occurs most often in urban communities, where it pertains to nearly 37 percent of the principals involved in merit pay programs.

Which of the following types of tenure do you have in your school district?

Tenure has long been an issue for principals and it has assumed particular importance during the past ten years, especially in those districts where teachers negotiate contracts and where declines in enrollment have led to reductions in force. If principals are credited with tenure not only as a principal but as a professional employee, they have seniority rights that would give them the option of returning to the classroom if they did not have adequate seniority to retain their position as a principal. If they have tenure rights only as administrators, however, they would be required to move to another district or to compete with other first-year applicants for any classroom teaching positions that might exist.

As for the situation that prevails today, half of K-8 principals do maintain tenure rights as a professional employee (see Table 61) of the district. About three in ten say that they maintain no tenure rights whatsoever, and two of ten have tenure rights only as principals.

TABLE 61—TYPES OF TENURE FOR PRINCIPALS

| Tenure | Total | Urban | Community Type | | Rural |
			Sub-Urban	Small Total	
None	28.2%	20.6%	18.0%	36.1%	36.6%
As a Principal	20.4	24.6	24.7	17.6	14.5
As a Professional Employee	51.4	54.9	57.2	46.3	48.8

What is your term of employment this year?

Most principals are on the job for 10 or 11 months per year.

More than half (54.3 percent) of today's K-8 principals are employed for 11 months or more (See Table 62), the first time that the proportion has ever topped the 50 percent level. An additional 40 percent work at least 10 but less than 11 months, a figure that is nearly 4 percent below that reported in 1978. These responses continue a trend, evident since at least 1968, toward longer work years among elementary and middle school principals.

The proportion of male principals who work less than 10 months is now greater (see Table 63) than that for their female counterparts (6 percent vs. 4.3 percent)—a switch

TABLE 62—ANNUAL TERM OF EMPLOYMENT OF PRINCIPALS
1968-1988

Months Employed	1968	1978	1988
9 but less than 10	21.4%	7.0%	5.7%
10 but less than 11	47.2	43.8	40.0
11 but less than 12	13.6	19.2	21.5
12	17.9	30.0	32.8

TABLE 63—ELEMENTARY PRINCIPAL'S TERM OF EMPLOYMENT IN 1987

| Month Employed | Total | Community Type | | | | Sex | |
		Urban	Sub-Urban	Small Town	Rural	Male	Female
9 but less than 10	5.7%	3.8%	4.6%	5.7%	8.6%	6.0%	4.3%
10 but less than 11	40.0	46.8	34.5	40.7	38.9	40.7	37.0
11 but less than 12	21.5	18.8	19.3	25.2	20.6	21.9	20.4
12	32.8	30.6	41.6	28.5	32.0	31.4	38.3

from 1978. Similarly, a higher percentage of women principals than men (58.7 percent to 53.3 percent) work an 11-month or longer year. Ten years ago, women were nearly twice as likely as men to work less than ten months, and only 40 percent of the women principals compared to 51 percent of the men worked 11 or more months. It appears that at least in regard to length of contract, gender equity has been achieved among elementary and middle school principals.

Just over half of urban principals are employed for less than 11 months, while 11 months is the minimum for more than half of all principals in rural, small town, and suburban communities. The longer contracts are found most frequently in suburban areas, where nearly 42 percent of the K-8 principals hold 12-month contracts and an additional 19.3 percent report working at least 11 months but less than 12.

 Does your school system give you a vacation? If yes, on what basis is the number of weeks established?

One month is the standard for vacation time.

Today about 63 percent of the nation's K-8 principals receive from one to eight weeks of vacation, while 37 percent report that they receive no vacation time at all (see Table 64). The mean vacation period is four weeks. More suburban (68.7 percent) and small town principals (64.8 percent) receive vacation time than do rural (59 percent) and urban (58.2 percent) principals.

Of the principals who receive a vacation, just over 45 percent indicate that it covers four weeks. A month off is the norm for 60 percent of the suburban principals (who tend to have longer average contracts) and about 40 percent of the principals in other types of communities. An additional 13.5 percent of the respondents receive a three-week vacation, while about 20 percent receive two weeks or less. At the other extreme, about 11 percent receive five weeks of vacation, 7.5 percent six weeks, and 2.8 percent either seven or eight weeks.

Three primary considerations go into determining how long a principal's vacation will be (see Table 65). The ma-

TABLE 64—PRINCIPAL VACATIONS PROVIDED BY THE SCHOOL SYSTEM

	Total	Urban	Community Type		Rural	Sex	
			Sub-Urban	Small Town		Male	Female
No	37.0%	41.8%	31.3%	35.2%	41.0%	37.4%	35.0%
Yes	63.0	58.2	68.7	64.8	59.0	62.6	65.0
1 week	2.4	2.0	1.2	4.1	2.3	2.1	3.5
2 weeks	17.5	15.7	9.8	20.3	30.2	16.5	21.1
3 weeks	13.5	17.6	7.3	17.6	14.0	13.4	14.0
4 weeks	45.2	41.2	59.8	35.1	39.5	46.4	40.4
5 weeks	11.1	13.7	12.2	10.8	4.7	12.4	7.0
6 weeks	7.5	5.9	7.3	8.1	9.3	6.7	10.5
7 weeks	2.4	3.9	2.4	2.7	0.0	2.6	1.8
8 weeks	0.4	0.0	0.0	1.4	0.0	0.0	1.8
Mean	04	04	04	04	03	04	04

TABLE 65—BASIS FOR NUMBER OF WEEKS OF VACATION FOR PRINCIPALS
(63.0% of respondents)

	Total	Urban	Community Type		Rural	Sex	
			Sub-Urban	Small Town		Male	Female
Dependent on length of tenure in district	17.5%	20.0%	25.0%	11.6%	14.3%	17.5%	16.8%
Dependent on length of contract	28.2	23.8	19.7	37.4	31.6	29.9	21.8
Standard for all principals	57.1	65.7	64.4	47.1	51.0	56.3	60.4
Other	6.5	6.7	3.0	8.4	8.2	5.6	9.9

(Respondents could select more than one option; this accounts for percent totals which exceed 100%.)

jority of principals (57.1 percent) are allocated a vacation that is "standard for all principals." This practice is particularly prevalent in urban (65.7 percent) and suburban communities (64.4 percent). For about one in three principals (28.2 percent) the vacation is "dependent on the length of contract," a practice that is more common in small towns (37.4 percent) and rural areas (31.6 percent). For another 17.5 percent, including 25 percent of the suburban and 20 percent of the urban principals, the amount of vacation is "dependent on length of tenure in district."

The annual vacation for an additional 6.5 percent of K-8 principals is determined by some "other" method. Although gender does not appear to be a factor in determining the amount of time principals receive, it may be worth noting that more females (9.9 percent) than males (5.6 percent) are in the "other" category.

What is the number of days you are on duty per year (exclusive of regularly paid holidays and paid vacation days)?

Some principals work over 240 days per year, some under 200.

The number of total days set forth in the contracts of K-8 principals varies widely (see Table 66). At the extremes, 10.4 percent work fewer than 200 days per year while 13.3 percent work in excess of 240. The number of specified contract days also tends to form clusters, the most popular being 200 to 204 days (12.4 percent), 210 to 214 days (16.4 percent), and 220 to 224 days (18.3 percent).

TABLE 66—PRINCIPAL DUTY DAYS PER YEAR
(EXCLUSIVE OF PAID HOLIDAYS AND VACATIONS)

		Sex		Degree Status	
Days on duty	*Total*	*Male*	*Female*	*Bach/Mast*	*6-Yr/Ph.D.*
Less than 200	10.4%	9.9%	12.8%	9.8%	11.7%
200 to 204	12.4	11.0	17.4	12.6	11.3
205 to 209	8.1	7.9	8.7	8.3	7.4
210 to 214	16.4	17.6	11.4	18.7	11.3
215 to 219	8.1	7.9	8.7	8.7	6.9
220 to 224	18.3	18.9	16.1	17.7	19.9
225 to 229	7.5	7.8	6.7	7.5	7.8
230 to 234	4.6	5.3	1.3	4.0	6.1
235 to 239	1.0	0.8	2.0	0.8	1.7
240 or more	13.3	12.9	14.8	11.9	16.0
Mean days worked	217	217	216	216	218

The mean number of days worked by K-8 principals is 217 and the median number is 215. For women and principals with the bachelor's or master's degree, the average is one day less than the average for principals as a whole. Men work an average of 217 days; principals who have a sixth year of preparation or a doctorate work 218.

Have you ever had a paid sabbatical leave as a principal?

Sabbaticals may exist but few get them.

In *Fringe Benefits for Administrators in Public Schools, 1985-86* (p. 13), the Educational Research Service reported that 53.7 percent of the school districts provide for sabbatical leaves for principals, a percentage that probably has not changed markedly since the study was conducted.

However, only 3.1 percent of K-8 principals have ever *received* such leave (see Table 67). The percentage of women reporting a sabbatical is 4.8 compared to 2.7 for men. Not unexpectedly, the most prevalent use of the sabbatical leave is reported by principals who have completed doctoral study—6.5 percent (a figure considerably lower than the 27 percent reported in 1978).

With the current emphasis on improving the skills of principals as instructional leaders, it seems curious that so few principals take advantage of sabbatical leave provisions to gain a more concentrated professional development experience.

Taking into consideration the time you typically arrive at school in the morning and leave in the afternoon, how much time (excluding evenings and weekends) do you spend at school each day?

Most principals are at school at least nine hours per day.

Nearly half (49.6 percent) of the nation's K-8 principals spend about nine hours at school each day, and for 30 percent it is ten hours. About 16 percent spend eight hours or less at school, and just over 4 percent spend an average of 11 or more (see Table 68).

The mean number of work hours per day is nine, the low being seven hours and the high 12. The work week for

TABLE 67—SABBATICAL LEAVES FOR ELEMENTARY PRINCIPALS

Used	Total	Sex		Degree Status	
		Male	Female	Bach/Mast	6-Yr/Ph.D.
Yes	3.1%	2.7%	4.8%	1.7%	6.5%
No	96.9	97.3	95.2	98.3	93.5

TABLE 68—TIME PRINCIPALS SPEND AT SCHOOL EACH DAY
(EXCLUDING EVENINGS AND WEEKENDS)

Hours Spent at School	Total	Sex	
		Male	Female
Less than 8 hours	1.1%	1.4%	0.0%
8 hours	14.6	14.5	15.2
9 hours	49.6	52.1	40.0
10 hours	30.4	27.6	41.2
11 hours	4.2	4.3	3.6
12 hours or more	0.1	0.2	0.0
Mean hours per day	09	09	09

more than 84 percent of K-8 principals exceeds the American "normal" of 40 hours.

 How many additional hours do you spend in school-related activities each week (exclude summers)?

The average work week for today's K-8 principals is 51 hours.

The number of additional hours K-8 principals spend at school each week ranges from one to 50, with a mean of six. Combining the mean responses to this question and the previous question, it appears that K-8 principals spend an average of 51 hours per week in school-related activities. This is an increase of six hours above the 45 hours per week average reported in 1978 (see Table 69).

The mean amounts of time vary by only one additional hour among the various comparison groups. As for where the extra time is most likely to occur, those groups reporting a mean of seven hours per week are principals with less than 14 years' experience, principals in schools with fewer than 400 students, principals in rural communities,

TABLE 69—ADDITIONAL HOURS SPENT IN SCHOOL-RELATED ACTIVITIES
EACH WEEK (EXCLUDING SUMMER)

Additional School-Related Hours	Total	Sex	
		Male	Female
Less than 2	3.2%	3.6%	1.3%
2	11.3	11.5	10.3
3	12.3	12.6	10.9
4	11.3	11.4	10.9
5	15.7	15.3	17.3
6-9	21.7	21.1	23.7
10-12	16.8	17.0	16.0
More than 12	7.7	7.5	9.6
Mean hours per week	06	06	07
Range—Low	01	01	01
High	50	50	20

female principals, principals less than 50 years of age, and those with the most academic preparation. Perhaps principals who have less experience (and are generally younger) require more time to accomplish some of the tasks expected of the principal. Those who are principals of smaller schools are least likely to have additional administrative support, and may need to spend this extra time just to keep up with the work load. Those in rural areas are more likely to administer schools with lower enrollment and may be expected to take on such additional responsibilities as assisting with coordination of transportation and supervision at athletic events. A higher percentage of women principals are found in the less experienced category and tend to have slightly smaller schools than men, which might explain why they spend an additional hour in school-related activities each week.

 What percent of your time do you estimate spending on each of the following responsibilities?

K-8 principals would appear to spend more than half of their time (53 percent) in three kinds of activity: supervision and evaluation of teachers, discipline and student management, and curriculum development.* The other half of their time is spread among parent/community contacts and duties, assigned by the central office, each of which takes up an average of 9 percent of the principal's week; facilities management, occupying an additional 8 percent of the principal's time; and 6 percent each on supervision/ evaluation of nonteaching staff, student evaluation/placement, and budget administration. "Other" activities absorb the remaining 2 percent.

NAESP's *Proficiencies for Principals* (p. 9) states that "the principal's highest priority . . . must be instructional leadership." At least as demonstrated by the amount of time they devote to this activity. K-8 principals have made that priority their own. The principals say that supervision and evaluation of teachers require at least 25 percent of their time, and more than one-third (except in the cases of principals of schools enrolling less than 400 students) say these activities consume at least 30 percent or more of their time. The study reveals a rather consistent (but not linear) relationship between the size of the school's enrollment and the percent of time the principals devote to this activity (see Table 70). Evidently, the larger the school the more time the principal spends on supervising and evaluating the teaching staff. Women are slightly more likely than men to concentrate on supervision and evaluation, as are principals with the greatest amount of academic preparation.

Discipline and student management command a mean of 17 percent of a principal's attention (see Table 71), though one in four say they spend less than 10 percent of their time on this activity. Principals with fewer than five years of experience report spending from 2 to 3 percent more time on discipline and student management than do their more experienced colleagues. Principals in both urban and small

---

* In previous studies no attempt was made to identify how principals actually use the time they spend in school. For the 1988 survey instrument, ten broad categories (nine specific areas plus an "other" category) were identified as the major areas in which principals might spend their time. Mean figures for the total responses are reported in Figure 7.

TABLE 70—TIME SPENT BY PRINCIPALS IN SUPERVISION/EVALUATION OF TEACHERS

Percent of Time Spent	Total	School Size			Sex		Degree Status	
		Less than 400	400-600	More than 600	Male	Female	Bach/ Mast	6-Yr/ Ph.D.
Less than 10	7.9%	10.3%	5.4%	7.9%	8.7%	5.1%	9.1%	5.4%
10-19	27.3	29.9	27.1	23.6	27.6	26.6	27.1	28.3
20-29	28.9	28.6	30.7	26.4	28.8	29.1	29.7	27.4
30 or more	35.9	31.2	36.8	42.1	35.0	39.2	34.1	39.0
Mean	25	24	26	26	25	26	25	26

TABLE 71—TIME SPENT BY PRINCIPALS IN DISCIPLINE/STUDENT MANAGEMENT

Percent of Time	Total	Years Experience			Community Type				Become Principal Again		Principalship Final Goal	
		Less Than 5	5 to 14	15 or More	Urban	Sub-Urban	Small Town	Rural	Cert/ Prob Would	Cert/ Prob Would Not	Yes	No
Less than 10 ..	26.3%	20.4%	27.4%	28.8%	22.7%	33.9%	22.7%	27.7%	27.4%	21.8%	28.7%	24.8%
10-19	33.7	35.2	31.5	36.0	36.0	33.9	32.8	31.9	35.1	26.6	32.3	34.5
20-29	22.5	23.5	24.1	19.6	20.9	21.2	24.4	22.3	22.0	23.4	23.7	21.2
30 or more	17.5	21.0	17.1	15.6	20.3	11.1	20.2	18.1	15.4	28.2	15.3	19.5
Mean	17	19	17	16	18	14	19	16	16	21	16	18

FIGURE 7—AVERAGE PERCENT OF DAY SPENT ON JOB RESPONSIBILITIES

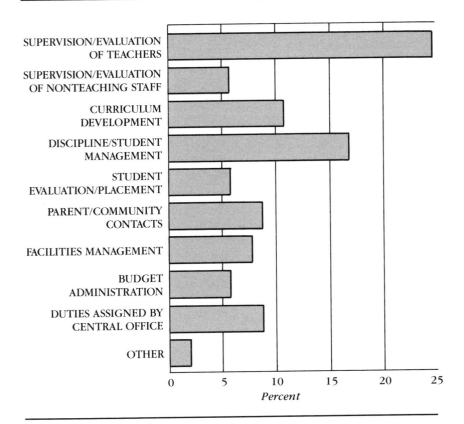

town communities also report spending 2 to 3 percent more time than the average for all principals, while those in suburban communities devote 3 percent *less* time. The discipline and student management function apparently has a strong bearing on the degree of satisfaction principals derive from their calling. Those who say they "certainly would" become a principal if starting over again, and those who see the principalship as their final goal, report spending only 16 percent of their time on these activities. Those who "certainly or probably would not" again become a principal spend 21 percent of their time (the highest of all of the comparison categories), and those who do not see the principalship as their final goal spend 18 percent.

The principals devote 11 percent of their time to curriculum development (see Table 72), another of the instructional leadership roles that has begun to receive particular attention in professional development programs in recent years. Mean scores in this area are distributed rather consistently across all subgroups, although principals with less than five years of experience give it only 9 percent of their time. Those who "certainly or probably would" choose to become principals again are almost twice as likely to spend at least 20 percent of their time in curriculum development.

TABLE 72—TIME SPENT BY PRINCIPALS IN CURRICULUM DEVELOPMENT

Percent of time	Total	Years Experience			Become Principal Again	
		Less Than 5	5 to 14	15 or More	Cert/ Prob Would	Prob Would Not
Less than 10	41.3%	51.2%	39.1%	39.2%	39.8%	47.6%
10-19	40.6	35.2	38.5	46.0	41.0	40.3
20-29	14.2	10.5	17.9	11.2	15.3	8.1
30 or more	3.9	3.1	4.4	3.6	3.9	4.0
Mean	11	9	11	10	11	10

SUMMARY

In general, principals hold a favorable view toward the conditions of their employment. About 88 percent are covered by some type of personal contract, with 36 percent holding a one-year agreement and 49 percent having some type of multiyear or continuing arrangement. Eighty percent also report having some type of written agreement that specifies salary, benefits, and working conditions. Half of the principals hold tenure as a professional employee in their district, although another 30 percent say they have no tenure rights whatsoever. Although sabbatical leaves are apparently available to at least half of the principals across the country, only 3 percent of the respondents in this study report having ever received such leave.

The mean 1987 salary reported in the study is $39,988, and for 17 percent of K-8 principals, the salary is tied to some type of merit or incentive pay system. For the first time ever, more than half of the principals report being employed 11 or more months, and the mean number of days worked is 217. The typical work day for principals is nine hours, and they spend an average of six additional hours per week in school-related activities outside the school day, making their typical work week total 51 hours.

More than half of a K-8 principal's time is consumed in three activities: supervision and evaluation of teachers, discipline and student management, and curriculum development. Supervision and evaluation of teachers demands the most time, typically consuming about one-fourth of the principal's day.

Chapter 6

Evaluation of Principals

I n discussing the uses and benefits of evaluation, NAESP's *Proficiencies for Principals* (p. 13) notes that "Proficient principals are well aware that the purposes and benefits of evaluation extend no less to themselves than to their students and teachers." With any evaluation there must of course be a foundation, a basis for measurement—a statement of what is expected of the persons being rated. Hence the 1988 survey posed (for the first time in this series of studies) the following question:

 Do you have a written job description with your school district for which you are held accountable and against which you are evaluated?

Today eight of ten K-8 principals have written job descriptions.

Eight out of ten of today's K-8 principals do have a written job description and are held accountable for carrying out its provisions (see Table 73). Nearly two of the eight principals say their job description may well differ from those of other principals in the district, having been tailored to their specific situation.

As for the 20 percent who do not have a written job description, it may be symptomatic that this figure includes a fourth of the respondents who would "certainly or probably not" become a principal if they were starting their careers over again.

 How often are you formally evaluated as a principal?

About 85 percent of elementary and middle school principals are formally evaluated (see Figure 8) at least once a

TABLE 73—PRINCIPALS' WRITTEN JOB DESCRIPTION FOR WHICH THEY ARE HELD ACCOUNTABLE AND AGAINST WHICH THEY ARE EVALUATED

		Become Principal Again	
	Total	*Certainly/ Probably Would*	*Certainly/Probably Would Not*
Do you have a written job description?			
Yes, standard for all principals	61.6%	62.1%	59.0%
Yes, different for each principal	18.7	19.5	16.4
No	19.7	18.4	24.6

FIGURE 8—FREQUENCY OF EVALUATION

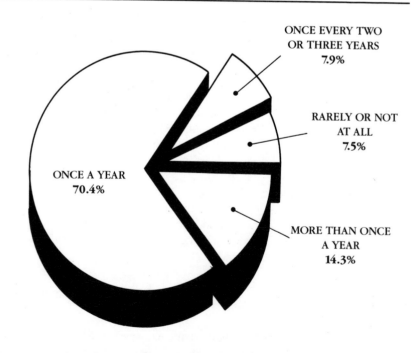

ONCE EVERY TWO OR THREE YEARS 7.9%

RARELY OR NOT AT ALL 7.5%

ONCE A YEAR 70.4%

MORE THAN ONCE A YEAR 14.3%

year—a figure that includes 14.3 percent who are evaluated *more* than once a year. Fifteen percent of the male principals are in the latter group, contrasted with only 11.5 percent of the female principals. Regardless of the number of years of experience or school enrollment, type of community, gender, age, or degree held, about 70 percent of today's K-8 principals are formally evaluated at least annually, versus 56 percent in 1978.

There are also principals—about 7.5 percent of the total—who are formally evaluated "rarely or not at all." They include 10.3 percent of the female principals and 10.4 percent of the principals in schools with enrollments of less than 400 pupils. The remaining 8 percent of the respondents report being evaluated once every two or three years.

A move would appear to have developed during the past decade toward evaluating principals more frequently. The trend is most evident when comparing the findings for principals who report being evaluated "rarely or not at all"—22 percent in 1978 vs. 7.5 percent today (see Table 74).

Is goal setting a routine part of your evaluation process?

Some 80 percent of K-8 schools formally establish goals.

The discipline of establishing goals is now seen as a basic element of the principal's job in 80 percent of the nation's K-8 schools (see Table 75). However, a breakdown by types of community clearly indicates that goal setting is far more often a part of the principal evaluation process in urban and suburban districts (87 percent each) than in small town (75 percent) or rural districts (70 percent).

TABLE 74—FORMAL EVALUATIONS OF PRINCIPALS: 1978, 1988

Frequency	1978	1988
More than one a year	12%	14.3%
One a year	56	70.4
One every 2-3 years	10	7.9
Rarely or not at all	22	7.5

TABLE 75—GOAL SETTING AS A PART OF PRINCIPAL EVALUATION

	Total	Urban	Community Type		Rural
			Sub-Urban	Small Town	
Yes	80.0%	87.1%	87.2%	74.9%	70.3%
No	20.0	12.9	12.8	25.1	29.7

From whom are opinions about your evaluation normally solicited?

Nowadays many people may play a principal evaluation role.

Of the wide range of people who may play a role in evaluating principals (see Table 76), the most frequent, in 72.5 percent of the cases, is the superintendent of schools—except in urban school districts. There only 45.9 percent of the principals say the superintendent gets directly involved. Urban principals report that an assistant superintendent is the most frequent participant (56.3 percent) and is joined in this process by other central office staff about as frequently as is the superintendent (43.7 percent).

About one-third of the principals say that their own opinions are a normal part of the evaluation process (an increase of more than 13 percent from 1978). That practice seems to be less common with experienced principals, which likely explains the slightly higher involvement of women in self-assessment than men. About 36.5 percent of the principals with less than five years of experience say they are asked to rate themselves, contrasted with 30.9 percent for those with more than 15 years of experience. About 29 percent of principals in rural and small towns say they are asked to make a self-assessment; among suburban principals the figure is more than 38 percent.

Teachers also figure frequently in the principal evaluation process, with 20 percent of the principals reporting their involvement, a 10 percent increase since 1978. Participation of teachers is most common in rural areas (27.9 percent) and least common in small towns (16.5 percent).

Also often considered are the opinions of parents (in 8.5 percent of the cases), students (4.2 percent), and "others" (5.7 percent).

TABLE 76—PARTICIPANTS IN PRINCIPALS' EVALUATION

| Participants | Totals | | | Community Type | | |
	1978	1988	Urban	Sub-Urban	Small Town	Rural
Superintendent	62.8%	72.5%	45.9%	69.2%	87.1%	83.7%
Assistant Superintendent	34.0	39.5	56.3	56.1	24.9	23.3
Other Central Office Personnel	25.5	24.8	43.7	28.3	10.8	20.3
Teachers	9.5	20.2	18.6	19.7	16.5	27.9
Parents	2.0	8.5	7.7	9.6	6.8	9.9
Students	1.3	4.2	2.7	4.0	4.0	5.8
Self	19.4	32.6	33.3	38.4	29.3	29.1
Others	7.2	5.7	7.7	3.5	4.0	8.1

Do you have the right to respond to your superiors after a formal evaluation?

Only 2.2 percent of the respondents say they are denied an opportunity to respond to their superiors following an evaluation. About 93 percent do have that right, and the remaining 4.8 percent say they aren't formally evaluated (see Table 77).

How frequently are you commended (by personal comment or in writing by the superintendent or other central office administrators) for something you have done as a principal?

Praise from higher-ups has become much more common.

Praise is of course a powerful motivator in dealing with pupils, and a trend seems to have emerged in recent years for principals to be on the receiving end. That proposition is demonstrated by a comparison of findings in the current study and the study of a decade earlier. About 18.7 percent of today's K-8 principals say they are praised "frequently," which is nearly a third more than in 1978, and about 47 percent are commended "sometimes," up from 42 percent. Meanwhile there has been a decline in the instances both of principals who say they are "seldom" commended and those who say "never," with the latter group dropping by more than 50 percent (see Figure 9) from a decade ago.

SUMMARY

Formal evaluations, conducted at least once a year, are reported by 85 percent of today's K-8 principals. Eighty percent of them say they have a written job description for which they are held accountable and against which they are evaluated. This same proportion of principals report formal goal-setting to be a standard part of the evaluation process, with the incidence being slightly more frequent in urban and suburban districts.

Except in urban districts, where an assistant superintendent usually takes the lead, the superintendent is the per-

TABLE 77—RIGHT TO RESPOND TO SUPERIORS AFTER A FORMAL EVALUATION

| | Total | Years Experience | | | Community Type | | | | Sex | |
		Less than 5	5 to 14	15 or More	Urban	Sub-Urban	Small Town	Rural	Male	Female
Yes	93.0%	90.4%	94.2%	93.3%	94.7%	93.6%	93.2%	89.8%	93.9%	88.9%
No	2.2	3.0	1.6	2.6	1.6	2.5	2.8	1.7	1.8	3.7
Not evaluated formally	4.9	6.6	4.1	4.1	3.7	4.0	4.0	8.5	4.2	7.4

FIGURE 9—FREQUENCY OF COMMENDATION

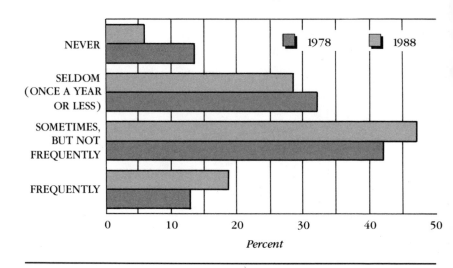

Percent

son most frequently involved in the evaluation of K-8 principals. About a third of the principals are called upon to evaluate their own performance, and about 98 percent say they have the right to respond to their superiors after a formal evaluation.

The study shows some increase over the last decade in the frequency with which principals are commended for doing a good job.

Chapter 7

Authority of the Principal

ne of the consistent findings in the Effective Schools research has been the degree to which the quality of a school's program is tied to the level of the principal's authority to make decisions governing the school's programs and operations. Having been given a high level of authority, the wise principal recognizes the capabilities and strengths of others and finds meaningful and appropriate ways to involve them in the decision-making process. With those kinds of considerations as a background, the study posed a series of questions that began with the following:

How would you describe the level of authority that principals in your district have to make *decisions concerning their schools?*

Nine out of ten K-8 principals say they are given "high" or "moderate" authority to run their schools (see Table 78). However, the apparent positiveness of that response is

TABLE 78—PRINCIPALS' PERCEIVED AUTHORITY TO MAKE DECISIONS
CONCERNING THEIR SCHOOL

Level of Authority	Total	Urban	Community Type Sub-Urban	Small Town	Rural	Sex Male	Female
High	49.0%	41.0%	50.2%	53.0%	51.4%	50.5%	42.4%
Moderate	41.4	45.7	39.8	40.3	39.4	40.7	44.8
Low	9.1	12.8	9.5	6.7	8.0	8.3	12.1
None	0.5	0.5	0.5	0.0	1.1	0.5	0.6

somewhat dampened by the fact that nearly one in ten principals report their level of authority to be "low" or "none." This situation most seriously afflicts principals in urban areas; theirs was the most negative response to having a "high" level of authority (only 41 percent) and the largest to the rating of "low" authority or "none" (13.3 percent). Women principals, constituting one-fourth of the respondents from urban areas, mirror this urban profile.

In general, is the authority to run your school given to you by the school board and central administration in balance with the degree to which they hold you responsible when things go wrong?

Responsibility is said to be in balance with authority.

About 81.6 percent of today's K-8 principals feel their authority and the performance expected of them are pretty well in balance. The percentages were even higher for men (83.4) and for principals with a doctorate or sixth year of study (86.8).

This same question was asked of principals ten years ago, and the responses then and now are much alike (see Table 79), with 80 percent of the 1978 principals responding "yes." Particularly noteworthy was the difference between the responses of urban principals and those from other types of communities. Just over 26 percent of the urban principals said "no," their authority and their responsibility are *not* in balance, whereas that response came from only about 15 percent of the principals from small towns and 16 percent of the suburban and rural principals.

Currently there is much talk about the promise for progress inherent in a transition from central-office management of the schools to site-based management. A major consideration in any such move is willingness by the central office to transfer appropriate autonomy and authority to the principal, and readiness by principals to understand and accept the proposition that such a transfer must be accompanied by accountability. Those were unfortunately considerations that the study could not measure.

TABLE 79—PRINCIPALS' PERCEIVED BALANCE OF AUTHORITY WITH RESPONSIBILITY

| | Total 1978 | Total 1988 | Urban | Community Type | | | Sex | | Degree Status | |
				Sub-Urban	Small Town	Rural	Male	Female	Bach/Mast	6-Yr/Ph.D.
Yes	80%	81.6%	73.9%	83.6%	84.8%	83.8%	83.4%	74.2%	79.3%	86.8%
No	20	18.4	26.1	16.4	15.2	16.2	16.6	25.8	20.7	13.2

What percent of the total money spent on your school this year (salaries, utilities, supplies, etc.) is subject to the discretionary authority of you and/or your staff?

In general, authority fails to extend to budget matters.

Their responses to the two lead-off questions suggest that in general, K-8 principals are pretty much in charge of things at their schools. When money enters the picture, however, their authority begins to seem more apparent than real. Overall, the typical K-8 principal controls only about 17 percent of the school's discretionary budget dollars (see Table 80), although women principals and those holding a sixth year or doctorate control 22 percent.

Nearly 20 percent of K-8 principals say they control "none" of the budget dollars, and an additional 53 percent say they control less than 20 percent. At the top end of this continuum, only 14 percent of the principals exercise discretionary authority over 50 percent or more of the total school budget. About 17 percent of rural principals say they have this much budget authority, about 12 percent of urban and small-town principals, and 14 percent of suburban principals.

Which of the following statements best describes your authority in each of these areas?

Principals have authority for supervising but not for hiring.

The study also sought indications of the principal's authority in three additional areas: selection of teachers, supervision and evaluation of staff, and instructional improvement in the school.

Selection of teachers is the area in which the fewest principals (about 37 percent) report having primary authority, and the only one of the three areas in which a significant number (about one in ten) suggest that they have "little or no authority" (see Figure 10). More than half (54 percent) of the principals report that they "share authority with central office" in the selection of teachers—a traditional practice that usually means that while principals may be invited to participate in interviewing candidates, final authority for selection and assignment rests with the central office. The larger the school system, the more centralized this process tends to become. Thus it is not surprising that nearly 17

TABLE 80—PERCENT OF TOTAL MONEY SUBJECT TO DISCRETIONARY
AUTHORITY OF PRINCIPAL AND/OR SCHOOL STAFF

| Percent | Total | Urban | Community Type | | Rural | Degree Status | |
			Sub-Urban	Small Town		Bach/Mast	6-Yr Ph.D.
None	19.5%	24.7%	17.7%	19.6%	16.8%	20.2%	17.3%
Less than 10	33.3	33.1	32.8	34.3	32.3	34.2	31.4
10-19	19.5	16.9	25.8	15.7	20.5	18.5	22.3
20-29	8.9	8.4	8.1	10.4	8.7	8.7	9.1
30-39	3.6	4.2	1.1	5.7	3.1	3.5	4.1
40-49	1.2	0.6	0.5	1.7	1.9	0.8	2.3
50 or more	14.0	12.0	14.0	12.6	16.8	14.2	13.6
Mean	17	16	17	17	19	21	22

FIGURE 10—PRINCIPALS' REPORTED AUTHORITY IN CERTAIN AREAS

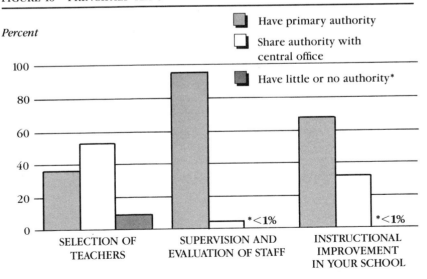

percent of urban principals say they have "little or no authority" in teacher selection. Nearly 10 percent of rural principals (compared to about 5 percent of the principals in small town and suburban communities) say they are in this same situation.

It is a paradoxical fact, then, that while principals are held predominantly accountable for the supervision and evaluation of teachers, they have relatively little authority over teacher selection. Nearly 96 percent of the principals in the study report that they have "primary authority" for supervising and evaluating teachers and almost none report "little or no authority." Only 4 percent of the principals say that central office staff gets involved in these areas.

Responsibility for improving the school's approach to instruction provides yet another measure of the principal's authority. Research clearly demonstrates that school improvement must originate within the individual school—it cannot successfully be imposed—and that the principal is the crucial figure in making improvement occur. Yet only 67.4 percent of the principals report having "primary authority" for improvement in their schools, with more female than male principals (74 percent vs. 66 percent) reporting themselves to be in this group. (It is quite possible that the 32 percent of principals who say authority is "shared with central office" largely reflects the fact that many of the factors involved in school improvement lie beyond the direct control of the building principal.)

The next ten years seem destined to be particularly exciting for principals, given the high priority that school improvement continues to receive on both state and national agendas. It is virtually inevitable that there will be some restructuring of schools during this time. The role of the building principal as a site-based manager is likely to become a pivotal part of such restructuring, a fact that has major implications for principal preparation programs.

 To what extent are teachers in your building involved in the development and evaluation of the instructional program?

Recent literature on school improvement has focused upon the importance of collegial involvement and the empowerment of teachers as being important factors in improving a school's effectiveness. It develops that a full range of teacher involvement in development and evaluation of the instructional program is to be found in today's K-8 schools (see Table 81).

About 61.5 percent of the principals say teachers have some "formal involvement" in developing and evaluating the instructional program. Such involvement was reported by about 65 percent of the suburban principals and 63 percent of those in small towns. Another 33.8 percent say their teachers have "no formal involvement but their opinions are solicited," an arrangement that apparently is most common in rural areas (36.2 percent).

About 1.1 percent of the respondents say teachers are "not at all" involved, apparently indicating that there are a few principals who continue to make decisions with little or no concern for the opinions of their teachers. And at the other extreme, 3.6 percent of the principals say that teacher involvement "consists solely of development and evaluation of program." Depending on how the respondents interpreted the question, this response could suggest that a few principals have abdicated their leadership responsibility for instructional improvement.

What is your role in evaluating teachers in your school?

Teacher evaluation, long recognized as one of the building principal's most important responsibilities, has received considerable emphasis in recent school improvement literature, and several states have mandated that principals re-

TABLE 81—EXTENT OF TEACHER INVOLVEMENT IN THE DEVELOPMENT AND EVALUATION OF THE INSTRUCTIONAL PROGRAM

	Total
Not at all	1.1%
No formal involvement but their opinions are solicited	33.8
Formal involvement	61.5
Process consists solely of development and evaluation of program by teachers	3.6

ceive special training in the evaluation process. Both in 1968 and in 1978, NAESP's ten-year surveys have included questions probing the extent of such evaluations and how frequently principals conduct them. However, no effort was made to determine the type of evaluation instrument used, nor the number of classroom observations typically included in the process. The 1988 study specifically referred to "narrative format" and "checklist format," and inquired into the number of classroom observations per teacher. The results are reported in Table 82.

Over the years there has clearly been an increased emphasis on teacher evaluation. As recently as 1968, 22 percent of all beginning teachers and 34 percent of all experienced teachers received no formal rating. By 1978 the incidence of no rating had declined dramatically—to only 6 percent for beginning teachers and 6.9 percent for experienced teachers. Currently it is less than 1 percent (.7) for beginning and experienced teachers alike.

In the conduct of these evaluations, both narrative and checklist formats are used extensively to record perfor-

TABLE 82—PRINCIPAL'S ROLE IN EVALUATING TEACHERS

Type of Evaluation Format	Beginning Teachers	Experienced Teachers
No formal evaluation	0.7%	0.7%
Narrative		
At least once a year	64.8	46.8
Every few years	1.0	19.1
Checklist		
At least once a year	55.1	38.5
Every few years	0.8	17.2
Average number of classroom visits/teacher		
One	1.5	22.3
Two	18.0	34.8
Three	27.0	16.1
More than three	46.7	19.1
No number specified	6.8	7.7

mance evaluations, with the narrative report being more common for both beginning and experienced teachers. Many principals employ both formats (explaining why the combined totals in Table 82 exceed 100 percent).

As for the number of classroom observations made with beginning and experienced teachers, 27 percent of the principals say they schedule three classroom visits for beginning teachers and an additional 46.7 percent schedule more than three. Less than 20 percent of the principals try to make do with two or fewer classroom observations with beginning teachers. There is less agreement about the number of observations that should be made when evaluating experienced teachers, except that it tends to be smaller for beginning teachers. More than 57 percent of the principals indicate one or two, another 16 percent say three, and 19 percent say more than three.

Does your school system have an "administrative team?"

"Administrative teams" are now common in most districts.

For purposes of the ten-year studies, the term "administrative team" is defined as "a structure or mechanism that attempts to bring the school system's administrative and supervisory personnel together for purposes of interaction, consultation, and decision making." More than seven of ten respondents to the 1988 study (71.5 percent) report working in school systems that use some type of administrative team (see Figure 11), a slight increase from the 68 percent reported in the 1978 study. While nearly 75 percent of suburban and small town principals are part of an administrative team, at least 30 percent of urban and rural principals are not.

A second part to this question was addressed to those who responded "yes," their school system does indeed have an administrative team arrangement. It asked them to describe the extent to which elementary principals are involved in this team. About nine of ten principals (89 percent) say they were involved "in a meaningful way" (see Figure 12). The other 10 percent say either that they are involved "in name only" (9.6 percent), are "not included" (1 percent), or that they "don't know" (.3 percent). When

FIGURE 11—ADMINISTRATIVE TEAM USED IN SCHOOL DISTRICT

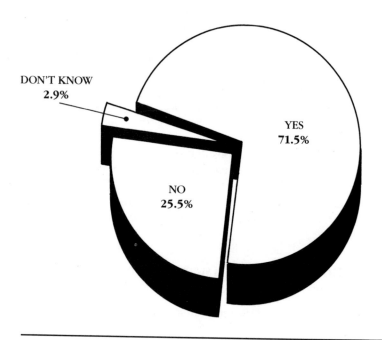

compared to the responses of ten years ago, 7 percent more K-8 principals perceive themselves as being "meaningfully involved" in an administrative team and 5 percent fewer than in 1978 perceive their involvement to be "in name only."

 How much influence do you think you have on school district decisions that affect elementary schools and elementary education?

Only 1 in 4 K-8 principals feel they have "much influence."

Slightly more than one in four K-8 principals (27.6 percent) believe they have "much influence" in school district decisions (see Table 83) that bear on K-8 education. About half (49.4 percent) feel they have "some influence" and the rest perceive themselves as having "little" (19.7 percent) or "no influence" (3.3 percent).

FIGURE 12—ELEMENTARY PRINCIPALS INCLUDED ON
THE ADMINISTRATIVE TEAM

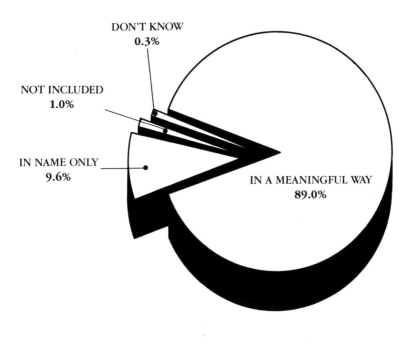

TABLE 83—PERCEIVED INFLUENCE OF PRINCIPAL ON SCHOOL DISTRICT
DECISIONS THAT AFFECT ELEMENTARY SCHOOLS AND
ELEMENTARY EDUCATION

			Community Type			Sex	
	Total	Urban	Sub-Urban	Small Town	Rural	Male	Female
Much influence	27.6%	13.2%	26.6%	32.9%	37.4%	28.8%	23.0%
Some influence	49.4	47.3	51.6	52.7	43.9	50.2	46.0
Little influence	19.7	30.8	18.8	14.0	17.0	18.2	26.1
No influence	3.3	8.8	3.1	0.4	1.8	2.8	5.0

Principals within the comparison groups tend to differ in their perceptions of the extent of their influence. Urban principals are about one-third as likely as rural or small town principals to perceive themselves as having "much influence" on such decisions, and one-half as likely as suburban principals. Women are more likely than men (31.1 percent vs. 21 percent) to feel they have "little or no influence." And perhaps it should be noted that the "much influence" response by principals with less than five years of experience (30.7 percent) declines steadily until it reaches only 26.8 percent of those with more than 15 years of experience.

SUMMARY

Eighty percent of K-8 principals feel that their authority to run their schools is in balance with the degree to which they are held responsible when things go wrong. They report controlling an average of 17 percent of the school-level budget dollars. About 96 percent say they have primary authority for staff supervision and evaluation. When it comes to selecting and hiring teachers, however, more than half say they "share authority with the central office" and nearly 10 percent say they have "no authority" at all. Nonetheless, about 68 percent of the principals report that they have primary authority for instructional improvement in their school.

There is some indication that K-8 principals are becoming more accepted as members of the school district administrative team. About 78 percent of the respondents report working in school districts where such a team approach is practiced, and nearly 90 percent of this group perceive their involvement as being "meaningful." Three of four principals believe they have "much or some influence" in district level decisions that affect elementary education.

Approximately 62 percent of principals say their teachers are formally involved in the development and evaluation of the school's instructional program.

Chapter 8

The Principal and Collective Bargaining

ollective bargaining has become a fact of life in the nation's schools during the past 20 years, bringing with it controversy and at times divisiveness both within and outside the profession. The questions addressed in this chapter focus on the reactions of K-8 principals to the collective bargaining process and their view of its effect on the quality of public education, on American public opinion, and on the salary and welfare of principals.

Q **Are the teachers in your school district covered by a collective bargaining contract?**

Most principals are in districts where teachers have negotiated contracts.

More than than seven out of ten K-8 principals work in a district in which teachers have collectively negotiated a contract (see Table 84), an increase of 3.1 percent from the 1978 study. Collective bargaining is reported most frequently by principals in suburban (78.2 percent) and urban (76.9 percent) schools, although nearly two out of three

TABLE 84—PRINCIPALS WORKING WITH TEACHERS WHO NEGOTIATE CONTRACTS

	Total 1978	Total 1988	Sex	
			Male	Female
Teachers negotiate	68.0%	71.3%	73.6%	61.6%
Teachers do not negotiate	32.0	28.7	26.4	38.4

principals in rural and small-town schools are also involved with management of a negotiated contract. A higher percent of males (73.6) than females (61.6) work in districts that have collective bargaining, a difference that may well arise from the fact that a high percentage of female principals are employed in the southwest and southeast parts of the country, where collective bargaining continues to be less common than in other sections.

 In your opinion, is collective bargaining by teachers having a good or bad effect on the quality of public education?

Criticism of teacher union bargaining may be waning.

There is some evidence that principals are getting inured to dealing with teacher unions. While 37 percent of them feel that collective bargaining by teachers has a bad effect on public education, that is a reduction from the 42.9 percent who felt that way ten years ago (see Table 85). Moreover, nearly 3 percent more (13.3 percent compared to 10.5 percent) say teacher collective bargaining has a "good effect." Almost 20 percent (compared to 16.5 percent in 1978) "don't know" what the effect is.

Male principals (32.7 percent) are more inclined to say that collective bargaining has "little if any effect" than are female principals (17.6 percent), while females are slightly more inclined to report a "bad effect" (41.8 percent vs. 36 percent) or to indicate they "don't know" (28.5 percent vs. 17.8 percent). By type of community, a greater proportion of urban (19.7) and suburban (16.3) principals say the effect is "good," yet 36.6 percent of the urban principals and 40.4 percent of those in suburbia say it is "bad." Only 10.2 percent of small town principals and 7.9 percent of those in rural schools see the effects of collective bargaining as "good." As the age of the respondents increases, so does their approval of collective bargaining. Those with a sixth year of education or a doctorate also feel slightly more favorable toward collective negotiations (16.5 percent "good effect") than do those with the bachelor's or master's degree (12.1 percent).

Since collective bargaining is a relatively new practice in education (it was not even mentioned in the 1968 study),

TABLE 85—EFFECT OF TEACHER NEGOTIATIONS ON QUALITY OF EDUCATION

| | Total 1978 | Total 1988 | Community Type | | | | Sex | | Age | | | Degree Status | |
			Urban	Sub-Urban	Small Town	Rural	Male	Female	40 or Less	41-50	Older than 50	Bachl. Mast	6-Yr/ Ph.D.
Good effect	10.5%	13.3%	19.7%	16.3%	10.2%	7.9%	13.5%	12.1%	10.3%	13.5%	15.4%	12.1%	16.5%
Little, if any effect	30.1	29.8	21.3	28.1	36.2	31.1	32.7	17.6	22.8	31.2	33.7	28.8	32.1
Bad effect	42.9	37.0	36.6	40.4	33.1	39.0	36.0	41.8	46.4	35.5	31.5	37.6	35.4
Don't know	16.5	19.9	22.4	15.3	20.5	22.0	17.8	28.5	20.5	19.9	19.5	21.5	16.0

responses reported in this study may reflect a growing accommodation to the process on the part of K-8 principals. There also seems to be a somewhat less militant stance on the part of teacher unions today than there was ten years ago, and the negative feelings on both sides would seem to be fading. Given the steady growth of collective bargaining by teachers across the country, the 56 percent turnover in principals that this study foresees during the next decade, and the fact that nearly all principals rise from the ranks of classroom teachers, it seems logical to suggest that ten years hence still fewer principals will feel that collective bargaining by teachers tends to have a "bad effect" on the quality of public education.

 In your opinion, is collective bargaining by principals having a good or bad effect on the quality of public education?

Feelings are less firm re bargaining by principals.

The Educational Research Service reported in *Teachers and Principals,* May 1984 (p. 67), that "about one-fourth of the principals are covered by a collectively bargained or negotiated agreement; 5.5 percent under the same agreement covering teachers and 18.1 percent under a separate contract." Since the 1978 NAESP study reported that only 22 percent of all principals collectively negotiated their contract, it is reasonable to assume that the percentages reported by ERS have not changed dramatically in the past three years.

Today's principals seem to have a slightly more favorable attitude toward collective bargaining by principals than by teachers (see Table 86). Just 13.7 percent say the effect on the quality of public education is "bad" (compared to 37 percent who feel that collective bargaining by teachers has a bad effect). On the other hand, only 8.1 percent see the effect as being "good," with 32.6 percent seeing "little if any effect" and 45.6 percent reporting that they "don't know." While some of this difference in opinion could be self-serving, it might also reflect the feeling that bargaining by principals is less disruptive to children's education because principals almost never strike.

TABLE 86—EFFECT OF COLLECTIVE BARGAINING BY PRINCIPALS
ON THE QUALITY OF PUBLIC EDUCATION

| | | Sex | | | Community Type | | |
	Total	Male	Female	Urban	Sub-Urban	Small Town	Rural
Good Effect	8.1%	8.9%	4.9%	11.0%	8.9%	8.5%	2.8%
Little, if any Effect	32.6	33.3	28.4	31.3	38.1	31.0	29.0
Bad Effect	13.7	14.0	13.0	12.1	9.9	14.5	19.3
Don't Know	45.6	43.8	53.7	45.6	43.1	46.0	48.9

In any event, the effect of collective bargaining by principals is seen as being "good" by 11 percent of urban principals, by 8.9 percent of suburban principals, and by 8.5 percent of those in small towns. Only 2.8 percent of their rural colleagues agree. A higher percentage of men (8.9 percent) than women (4.9 percent) view such collective bargaining as "good." About 44 percent of the men and 54 percent of the women say they "don't know."

A further indication of waning antagonism may lie in the survey's finding that those persons who have moved into the principalship within the past five years are more favorable toward collective bargaining by principals (10.7 percent report a "good effect") than those who have been in the principalship for longer periods of time, though over half of this group (51.2 percent) "don't know" what the effect is.

 What, in your opinion, has been the effect of collective bargaining by principals on the salary and welfare of principals?

Few principals feel collective bargaining has helped them.

Principal enthusiasm for collective bargaining by principals, never more than tepid at best, seems to be cooling even further (see Table 87). Only 15.8 percent feel the process had a "good effect" on their welfare, and that figure is 7 percent below the rating of a decade ago. A "bad effect" was reported by 22.6 percent fewer of the respondents than in 1978, those saying "little if any effect" increased 28

TABLE 87—EFFECTS OF COLLECTIVE BARGAINING BY PRINCIPALS
ON THE SALARY AND WELFARE OF PRINCIPALS

	Total 1978	Total 1988	Years Experience		
			Less Than 5	5- 14	15 or More
Good effect	22.8%	15.8%	15.0%	14.9%	18.3%
Little, if any effect	29.3	33.5	29.3	34.0	35.7
Bad effect	5.5	6.9	6.0	8.3	4.6
Don't know	42.4	43.7	49.7	42.8	41.4

percent, and those responding "don't know" increased by
1.3 percent. "Don't know" is in fact the most common reply
to the question, and it is in particular the response of the
principals with the least experience.

**What effect, in your opinion, is collective bargain-
ing in public education having on public opinion
generally?**

*Bargaining by
educators is felt
to have a poor
PR effect.*

More than half (55.7 percent) of today's K-8 principals believe that public opinion toward public education is ad-
versely affected by collective bargaining in public education (see Table 88), a slight decrease in the "bad" rating
from the 62 percent who gave that response a decade ago.
Only 4.1 percent see the effect as being "good," and 23 per-

TABLE 88—GENERAL EFFECT OF COLLECTIVE BARGAINING IN
PUBLIC EDUCATION ON PUBLIC OPINION

	Total 1978	Total 1988	Sex		Age		
			Male	Female	40 or Less	41- 50	Older than 50
Good effect	3.3%	4.1%	4.7%	1.8%	2.2%	4.6%	4.9%
Little, if any effect	20.3	23.0	24.5	15.9	16.1	22.5	29.3
Bad effect	62.0	55.7	55.0	58.5	63.4	56.6	48.5
Don't know	14.4	17.3	15.7	23.8	18.3	16.3	17.3

cent feel it has "little if any effect." Women in this study were slightly more united in their negative view toward collective bargaining than were the men. Contrary to what some might expect, principals age 40 or less were most likely to see the effect as "bad," whereas the attitude of the two older groupings were progressively more favorable.

There appears to be a continuing concern among elementary and middle school principals that collective bargaining by teachers and principals exerts a negative effect on public opinion. The extent of this concern is suggested by the clear majority in every subset of the study who see the effect as being "bad."

Have you personally been through a teachers' strike in the last five years?

Few principals have had direct experience with teacher strikes.

Although teacher strikes receive a great deal of news media attention, and inevitably are disruptive, 88.6 percent of K-8 principals have not had firsthand involvement in such an event during the past five years (see Table 89). Of those who have, 8.9 percent had the experience as a principal, 1.2 percent as a teacher, and 1.6 percent in some other position. The greatest proportion were from suburban (14.8 percent) and urban (10.7 percent) communities.

If yes, did your school district attempt to remain open during the strike?

One of the most difficult and frequently divisive decisions a district faces during a strike is whether to attempt to keep

TABLE 89—EXPERIENCE WITH TEACHERS' STRIKE IN LAST FIVE YEARS

				Community Type		
	Total 1978	Total 1988	Urban	Sub-Urban	Small Town	Rural
Yes, as a Principal	16%	8.9%	10.7%	14.8%	7.0%	2.8%
Yes, as a Teacher	2	1.2	3.2	0.5	0.4	1.1
Yes, in another position	1	1.6	2.7	0.0	2.3	1.1
No	81	88.6	84.5	84.7	90.2	94.9

the schools open. Of the 8.9 percent of K-8 principals who experienced a strike during the past five years, 62 percent said they sought to keep the schools open, a decision reported most frequently by suburban principals (65.5 percent) and least frequently by those in small towns (56.3 percent).

SUMMARY

More than 70 percent of principals in the United States work in districts in which teachers bargain collectively. Principals tend to feel that teacher negotiations have a negative impact on the quality of education, with 42.9 percent saying the practice has a "bad effect" while another 20 percent "don't know." They are slightly more positive about the effects of *principal* collective bargaining, with only 14 percent reporting a "bad effect," while another 46 percent say they "don't know" what the effect is. The majority of principals see little advantage to collective bargaining by principals so far as their salary and general welfare are concerned. Overall, about 58 percent of principals feel that in general, collective bargaining in public education has a "bad effect" on public opinion.

A strike by teachers was experienced by less than 12 percent of the principals in the study, and more than 60 percent of them sought to keep their schools open.

Chapter 9

Issues and Problems Before the Principal

The past decade has been a time of extraordinary change for elementary and middle school principals. No period in the history of education, even the "golden years" that followed the launching of Sputnik, has witnessed such an intense focus on school operations and program quality as that touched off by the publication in 1983 of the U.S. Department of Education's *A Nation At Risk: The Imperative for Educational Reform*. Issued under the auspices of then Secretary of Education T. H. Bell, *A Nation At Risk* not only had an enormous impact in and of itself but touched off half a hundred additional reports, each focusing on promoting the specific agenda of the sponsor as a way to improve the nation's schools.

The impact of these reports (and the actions they generated) came swiftly, and was astonishing in its scope. The call for change, largely rooted in a return to a solid intellectual and academic focus and heavily promoted as being necessary to the nation's economic and political survival, resulted in the enactment of a range of new state mandates. These focused in particular on the preparation of teachers and school administrators, but they also involved a number of modifications in the operation and curriculum of individual schools and school districts. The jury is still out on what the long-term effect of these imposed mandates will be, and a verdict may not be forthcoming until the kindergarten class of 1988-89 becomes the first graduating class of the 21st century.

Many positive outcomes can be expected both from the initiatives of recent years and from the modifications that will continue to be made during the next decade. Change can be beneficial, and indeed as NAESP's *Standards for Quality Elementary Schools* notes:

> Quality schools are never satisfied that all is well. They are continually seeking to improve, to find better ways of meeting the changing needs of their students and the communities in which they are located (p. 2).

At any rate, through all of the upheaval and uncertainty that change engenders, elementary and middle school principals must "keep school." They must work with the students who are in their classrooms, the teachers who are already on their staffs, the existing curriculum. They must face the reality of changing home and family structures, societal pressures, limited financial resources, and the host of other problems that are present in today's schools.

That is the background against which the study sought responses to the following series of questions:

 In your opinion, has the role of the principal in relation to the following areas changed in the last five years?

K-8 principal role appears to be broadening.

Much attention has been given recently to seven particular aspects of the principal's role: 1) building level authority and responsibility; 2) curriculum development; 3) development of instructional practices; 4) fiscal decision making; 5) personnel selection; 6) personnel evaluation; and 7) participation in district policy development. In the responses for each of these areas, the principals were asked to note either that there had been an "increase" in their responsibility over the past five years or "no change" or a "decrease."

More than half of the respondents reported increases in four of the seven areas and no change in the other three (see Table 90). Six out of ten (60.5 percent) cite evaluation of personnel as the area that has changed most. Possibly because of its close conceptual link with evaluation, development of instructional practices ranks second (57 percent), followed by curriculum development (52.4 percent)

TABLE 90—PERCEPTIONS OF PRINCIPALS REGARDING AREAS OF CHANGING
RESPONSIBILITIES DURING THE PAST FIVE YEARS

	Total
Building Level Authority/Responsibility:	
Increase	51.1%
No change	34.1
Decrease	14.8
Curriculum Development:	
Increase	52.4
No change	35.2
Decrease	12.4
Development of Instructional Practices:	
Increase	57.0
No change	35.0
Decrease	7.9
Fiscal Decision Making:	
Increase	27.0
No change	56.6
Decrease	16.4
Personnel Selection:	
Increase	29.2
No change	58.8
Decrease	12.0
Personnel Evaluation:	
Increase	60.5
No change	38.5
Decrease	1.0
Participation in District Policy Development:	
Increase	26.6
No change	60.0
Decrease	14.3

and building level authority and responsibility (51.1 percent). In responses by subgroups, only 46 percent of the principals who hold the doctorate agreed with this perception, and the latter three changes evidently are felt most by principals from small town and rural communities. Less than half of the suburban and urban principals say their roles in curriculum development have changed, and just 46 percent of the suburban principals report increase in building level authority and responsibility.*

Although more than half of the respondents perceive "no change" in their roles in connection with developing district policy (60 percent), personnel selection (58.8 percent), or fiscal decision making (56.6 percent), there are indications that change may nevertheless be underway. Nearly 30 percent of the respondents say their role in personnel selection has increased during the past five years, and 27 percent say they have greater responsibilities in fiscal decision making and in the development of district policy.

 Have you ever been named in a civil suit related to your position as principal?

More than one principal in ten has been named in a civil suit.

A major concern of principals everywhere in the United States is the financial hardship that could result from a civil suit related to their position as principal. In the responses to these questions may be found both good and bad news for elementary/middle school principals (see Table 91). The relatively good news is that "only" 12.5 percent of the survey's respondents report ever having been named in such a suit. Suburban (14.8 percent) and urban (12.8 percent) principals are more often confronted by this problem than are principals from rural areas (11.9 percent) and small towns (10.6 percent). Also males (13.4 percent) are also more likely than females (9 percent) to be named in such suits.

---

* Data presented in Chapter 7 provide further evidence that these are areas in which principals now devote more time and attention.

The numbers involved are too small to permit reliable judgments, but it is illuminating to examine the types of complaints filed and the outcomes. Although nearly one in five civil cases (18.4 percent) are reported to be still in progress, nearly 42 percent of such suits are reportedly dropped and 15.5 percent are settled in favor of the principal; only 1 percent are reported to have resulted in a judgment against the principal. The bad news is that more than one in ten principals (the same 12.5 percent as above) has been put through the personal trauma that goes with being named in a civil suit.

The most frequent complaint lodged against principals is liability for student injury (49.6 percent). Nearly 60 percent of suburban principals involved in a civil suit have faced this kind of charge. The safety and proper supervision of students is clearly a critical matter. One in five principals involved in a civil suit (20.3 percent) reports being named as a result of dismissing a member of the staff—an action that generated 32.1 percent of the suits against urban principals and 12.8 percent among suburban principals. An additional 13 percent of such principals are named to civil suits for "reporting suspected child abuse" (12.2 percent) or "failure to report suspected child abuse" (.8 percent). Principals involved in either of these situations face a potential "lose-lose" dilemma. Failure to dismiss incompetent faculty means poor educational experiences for large numbers of children and continuing problems for the principal, but failure to follow "due process" procedures and to have on file appropriate documentation to support such action opens the door to civil action. A requirement to report child abuse has been mandated in most states, but doing so obviously can produce a backlash.

Women were about three times as likely as men to be among the 13.8 percent of principals to have "other" complaints filed against them—such things as liability for injury to a parent or other visitor, suspension or expulsion of a student, and participation on an employment selection committee in which a violation of civil rights is charged.

When faced with a civil suit, the majority of principals (58.2 percent) report receiving formal support from the school district as a first step. Such is the case with over 70 percent of suburban principals, but only 52.4 percent for

TABLE 91—EXPERIENCES OF PRINCIPALS WITH CIVIL SUITS

	Total	Community Type				Sex		Become Prin. Again	
		Urban	Sub-Urban	Small Town	Rural	Male	Female	Cert/Prob Would	Cert/Prob Would Not
Have you ever been named in a civil suit related to your position as principal?									
Yes	12.5%	12.8%	14.8%	10.6%	11.9%	13.4%	9.0%	11.7%	15.8%
No	87.5	87.2	85.2	89.4	88.1	86.6	91.0	88.3	84.2
***To what was the complaint related?**									
Liability for student injury	49.6	42.9	59.0	42.9	46.2	50.5	44.4	52.1	42.3
Liability for staff member	1.6	-	2.6	-	3.8	1.9	-	2.1	-
Dismissal of staff member	20.3	32.1	12.8	21.4	19.2	21.0	16.7	19.1	23.1
Provision of educational services	1.6	-	2.6	3.6	-	1.9	-	2.1	-
Reporting of suspected child abuse	12.2	10.7	7.7	14.3	19.2	13.3	5.6	10.6	15.4
Failure to report suspected child abuse	.8	-	-	3.6	-	1.0	-	-	3.8
Other	13.8	14.3	15.4	14.3	11.5	10.5	33.3	13.8	15.4

*What was the outcome?

Suit dropped	41.7	50.0	43.3	30.8	42.9	44.3	26.7	43.0	38.1
Settled out of court	23.3	12.5	33.3	26.9	19.0	22.7	26.7	21.5	23.8
Case still in progress	18.4	20.8	13.3	23.1	14.3	15.9	33.3	20.3	14.3
Judgment in my favor	15.5	16.7	6.7	19.2	23.8	15.9	13.3	15.2	19.0
Judgment against me	1.0	-	3.3	-	-	1.1	-	-	4.8

*From whom did you get formal support?

School district	58.2	52.4	70.3	53.8	57.6	56.5	68.2	59.0	54.5
Local administrator association	7.2	14.3	-	5.1	9.1	7.6	4.5	7.7	6.1
State administrator association	7.8	7.1	2.7	12.8	9.1	8.4	4.5	7.7	9.1
National administrator association	2.6	4.8	-	2.6	3.0	2.3	4.5	1.7	6.1
Insurance company	20.9	21.4	21.6	20.5	18.2	21.4	18.2	21.4	18.2
None of the above	3.3	-	5.4	5.1	3.0	3.8	-	2.6	6.1
Number responding	830	188	203	255	177	662	166	681	133

*The numbers responding to sub-questions are small; the data is included only to provide a baseline for future comparison.

urban principals and about 54 percent for principals in small towns. Nearly 21 percent of the respondents received formal support from an insurance company, a figure that was consistent among all subgroups. Among the total respondents, 7.8 percent report receiving support from their state association, 7.2 percent from their local association, and 2.6 from their national administrator association. Although the latter figures appear lower than might be expected, the reason lies in the fact that liability assistance by administrator associations comes on top of assistance covered by the local school district or its insurance carrier.

The financial aspects of being sued represent, of course, only a part of the story. Principals who are confronted by a civil action also undergo considerable personal anguish, simply from being named in a suit. Thus perhaps it is not surprising that among the principals who have been named in a civil suit, 15.8 percent say they "certainly/probably would not choose to become a principal if starting over again." Although 38 percent of the suits against those same respondents were dropped and 19 percent settled in their favor, they also experienced the highest percent (4.8) of cases that resulted in a judgment against them.

To what extent is each item listed below currently or potentially (within the next year) a problem in the school for which you are now responsible?

The number one challenge: programs for underachievers.

The list cited in the question contained 36 entries (see Table 92), and the principals were asked to rate each as being "major" or "minor" or "little or no" problem at all.

Only four were rated as being "major" problem areas by as much as 20 percent of the respondents. Ranked from high to low, they were 1) providing programs for underachievers; 2) coping with state regulations and initiatives; 3) effectively meshing instruction with special academic programs; and 4) level of parent involvement. Fifteen of the areas were seen as "little or no" problem by more than 50 percent of the principals. In general it would appear that while elementary and middle school principals are faced

TABLE 92—PROBLEMS THE PRINCIPAL FACES

	TOTALS Major/ Minor	Major Only >10%
Providing programs for underachievers	74.3%	(1) 29.4%
+Managing student behavior	70.8	(6) 18.8
Coping with state regulations/initiatives	70.7	(2) 22.5
Evaluating teachers	70.2	(5) 19.7
+ +Level of parental involvement	70.1	(4) 20.8
Level of teacher performance	69.4	(12) 15.1
Providing programs for gifted and talented students	66.9	(7) 18.5
Effectively meshing routine classroom instruction with special academic pull-out programs	65.7	(3) 21.7
Child abuse	64.6	(18) 11.6
+Pupil absenteeism	64.4	(14) 13.3
Staff morale	61.0	(13) 13.6
Special needs of latchkey kids	61.0	(10) 16.7
+Dismissing incompetent staff	56.9	(9) 17.7
Inadequate availability of computers, video machines, etc. for instruction	56.8	(11) 15.7
Teacher absenteeism	54.6	
Crisis management	52.4	
Providing programs for handicapped learners	50.8	(17) 11.8
+Increasing enrollment	50.6	(8) 18.4
Coping with federal regulations	49.7	
Complying with student records regulations	37.8	
Central office involvement with school building decisions	47.7	
Changing composition of student body	44.6	(16) 12.1
Declining test scores	44.5	
Teachers union activities	43.6	
Increased interest in pre-kindergarten program	42.5	(19) 11.6
Vandalism	40.2	
Declining enrollment	39.0	(15) 12.6
Sexual behavior of pupils	36.2	
Use of drugs by pupils	35.3	
Teacher shortages	34.3	
Use of alcoholic beverages by students	28.2	
Non-English speaking students	27.0	
Censorship of textbooks by segments of the public	26.3	
Violence in the schools	23.8	
Use of alcoholic beverages by staff	19.4	
Strike management	15.4	

+ = Urban problem (+ > 8%)
+ + = Urban problem (+ > 10%)

with a wide variety of problems, very few are consistently perceived as being of major potential.*

Two of the problem areas that fall in the top half of the combined totals —teacher absenteeism and crisis management—were not perceived to be "major" problems by at least 10 percent of the respondents. Within the bottom half of the combined responses, however, are three areas that *are* perceived as "major" problems by more than 11 percent of the principals. These areas, and the percent of principals who see them as presenting major problems, are declining enrollment (12.6 percent), changing composition of the student body (12.1 percent), and increasing interest in prekindergarten programs (11.6 percent).

The "major" responses of urban principals were substantially higher for seven of the problem areas than those by principals from the other types of communities. These areas and the difference in percent of "major" responses are level of parent involvement (10.9 percent), managing student behavior (9.8 percent), pupil absenteeism (8.9 percent), dismissing incompetent staff (8.2 percent), changing composition of the student body (7.5 percent), declining test scores (6.4 percent), and crises management (6.1 percent). The higher scores in these areas provide an indication of the unique administrative and educational problems faced by principals of urban schools. The only area in which the "major" response from urban principals was at least 6 percent lower than that for the group as a whole was that of coping with state regulations and initiatives.

Some interesting differences also emerge from a comparison of the responses from principals who "certainly/probably would become a principal again" with those who certainly or probably would not do so. Seven areas showed at least 6 percent differences in responses between these respondent groups. For those who would not become a principal again, these seven areas (and the percentage dif-

* For Table 92 the percentages of responses for both "major" and "minor" problems were added together to provide a rank order. So that the combined ratings might be compared with just the "major" ratings, the table also indicates all "major" percentage totals that exceed 10 percent and the rank that the problem would have been given on the basis of this single ranking.

ference in reporting them as "major" problems) are coping with state regulations and initiatives (15.6 percent), managing student behavior (11 percent), dismissing incompetent staff (9.4 percent), level of teacher performance (8.8 percent), evaluating teachers (8.1 percent), teacher absenteeism (8 percent), and staff morale (6.1 percent). Thus it would appear that the principals who are most discontent with their job believe that the problems emerging from recent "reform" regulations and initiatives, combined with the persistent problems associated with management of teachers and student behavior, are making the principal's job more difficult and less personally satisfying.

There are two additional areas in which differences of at least 6 percentage points are to be noted within a comparison group. "Major" responses by female principals exceed by 6.5 percent the total group responses regarding the special needs of latchkey children, and are 8.2 percent higher than the responses of their male colleagues. The data do not reveal whether female principals tend to be assigned to schools that have more latchkey children, nor is it clear whether this difference is an indication of greater sensitivity on the part of women to such childhood problems.

Relative to your own feelings of job security, to what extent is each of the items listed currently or potentially (within the next year) a problem?

Security appears to be a major concern for K-8 principals.

Nine items were identified (see list in Table 93) which were judged likely to have major impact on the principal's feelings relative to job security. The principals were asked to rate each item as presenting a "major," "minor," or "little or no" problem so far as job security is concerned.

Elementary and middle school principals would appear to feel relatively secure in their job (see Table 93). Only one area, "unsatisfactory student performance," is viewed as having a a "major" effect on their sense of security by more than one in five (21.8 percent). Thirty percent of urban principals report this as a "major" sense of security problem, while only 18 percent of suburban and 18.6 percent of small town principals feel this way. Of the principals who certainly or probably would not become a principal if

TABLE 93—EXTENT TO WHICH EACH OF THE ITEMS LISTED IS CURRENTLY OR POTENTIALLY (WITHIN THE NEXT YEAR) A PROBLEM RELATED TO JOB SECURITY

	Total	Community Type				Sex	
		Urban	Sub-Urban	Small Town	Rural	Male	Female
Unsatisfactory student performance:							
Major	21.8%	30.3%	18.0%	18.6%	22.3%	22.3%	20.2%
Minor	42.5	40.0	40.0	42.9	46.8	43.8	36.8
Little or no	35.7	29.8	42.0	38.5	30.9	33.9	43.0
Conflicts with teachers:							
Major	8.0	9.8	6.0	7.8	9.2	7.6	9.9
Minor	48.9	48.8	50.0	45.7	52.0	51.1	39.2
Little or no	43.0	41.3	44.0	46.5	38.8	41.3	50.9
Conflict between my philosophy and that of superintendent:							
Major	11.2	9.1	9.6	11.2	14.6	11.7	9.2
Minor	37.5	37.1	35.7	40.4	36.3	40.2	27.2
Little or no	51.3	53.8	54.8	48.4	49.0	48.2	63.6
Conflict between my philosophy and that of parents:							
Major	6.0	5.9	7.0	5.9	5.1	6.5	3.7
Minor	42.7	42.2	40.4	43.0	45.2	43.8	38.3
Little or no	51.3	51.9	52.5	51.0	49.7	49.7	58.0

Lack of liability insurance:							
Major	5.4	7.6	5.1	3.2	6.8	6.1	2.5
Minor	25.0	22.2	26.9	24.4	25.8	26.1	20.1
Little or no	69.7	70.2	68.0	72.4	67.4	67.7	77.4
Reduction in force due to declining enrollment:							
Major	11.3	7.6	11.1	11.6	14.9	11.6	9.3
Minor	25.0	23.0	27.3	24.7	25.3	27.0	17.5
Little or no	63.7	69.4	61.6	63.7	59.8	61.4	73.1
Reorganization of schools in district:							
Major	13.3	11.4	14.6	12.0	16.0	13.5	12.5
Minor	23.7	25.5	24.2	21.5	23.4	23.6	23.2
Little or no	63.0	63.0	61.1	66.5	60.6	63.0	64.3
Poor personal performance evaluation:							
Major	5.2	5.7	4.6	4.8	5.8	5.7	3.1
Minor	21.1	18.1	21.8	21.7	23.1	24.1	8.1
Little or no	73.7	80.9	73.6	73.5	71.1	70.3	88.8
Personal deficiencies in skill areas:							
Major	3.5	4.0	3.6	2.5	4.0	4.0	1.3
Minor	29.8	26.8	29.0	30.5	33.1	31.2	23.1
Little or no	66.7	69.3	67.4	67.0	62.8	64.7	75.6

starting over again, one in four (26.1 percent) also see this as a "major" problem. Since the question was framed in the context of job security, it would appear that many of today's principals are experiencing considerable pressure to bring about significant and visible student performance—most likely as reflected in scores on standardized tests. It is not clear from these data whether such pressure is self-imposed or the result of external forces.

Three additional problem areas are viewed by more than 10 percent of the participants as having a "major" impact on their sense of job security. District reorganization of the schools is viewed as such a problem by 13.3 percent of K-8 principals, being most frequently reported by those in rural (16 percent) and suburban schools (14.6 percent). Reduction in force due to declining enrollment is seen as a job-security problem by 11.3 percent of the respondents, particularly those in rural areas (14.9 percent), contrasted with those in cities (only 7.6 percent). The third "major" problem area in this category, "conflict between my philosophy and that of the superintendent," was reported by a total of 11.2 percent of the respondents. Rural principals (14.6 percent) again seem most likely to find themselves in this kind of situation, while urban (9.1 percent) and suburban principals (9.6 percent) are least likely.

The generally positive feelings principals report relative to job security may best be summarized by looking at the two areas that relate most specifically to personal performance. Nearly three out of four principals see "little or no" problem with their performance evaluation, and two of three report "little or no" personal deficiencies in skill areas. Only 5.2 percent of the total respondents report poor personal performance evaluation as a "major" problem, and even fewer (3.5 percent) report personal deficiencies in skill areas. Clearly, elementary and middle school principals perceive themselves to be competent in their administrative skills and are confident in the quality of their leadership. As a result, they feel relatively secure in their jobs.

SUMMARY

More than half of today's K-8 principals feel that there has been an increase during the past five years in their role in personnel evaluation, development of instructional practices, curriculum development, and building level authority and responsibility. That the principalship is far from being a static position is demonstrated by the heavy impact on building level principals of the array of school reform activities during the past five years.

Although a litigious climate exists throughout the country, only 12.5 percent of principals have had to face a civil action, and just 1 percent of these cases has resulted in a judgment finding against the principal. Liability for student injury is the basis for nearly half of all civil suits filed against K-8 principals, with teacher dismissal cases generating an additional 20 percent. Although the number of civil suits and judgments against principals is relatively small, the evidence suggests that those who have to face even the prospect of such action find the price a high one, personally as well as professionally.

Of 36 areas identified as posing current or potential problems, only four are viewed by more than one in five principals as being "major." They are providing programs for underachievers, coping with state regulations and initiatives, effectively meshing instruction with special academic programs, and the level of parent involvement. Problems such as managing student behavior, evaluating teachers, and level of teacher performance were ranked in the top six areas when combining "major" and "minor" ratings of principals. Urban principals identified somewhat different problems as priorities, with parent involvement, managing student behavior, pupil absenteeism, dismissing incompetent staff, and increasing enrollment as their top five concerns.

Of the nine items identified as likely to have major impact on the principal's feelings relative to job security, only "unsatisfactory student performance" was reported to be of "major" concern to more than 20 percent of principals. More than one in ten principals also cited "reorganization of schools in the district," "reduction in force due to declining enrollment," and "conflict between my philosophy and that of the superintendent" as major problem areas. In general, elementary and middle school principals appear to be confident of their skills and their ability to perform on the job, and feel relatively secure in their positions

Chapter 10

The Future of the K-8 Principalship

In examining the current status of the elementary school principalship in the United States, and comparing current conditions with those of the past, the preceding chapters provide a glimpse into the future by suggesting conditions and trends that are likely to have an impact on the principalship in the years ahead. Those trends might well include the following:

1. *A 50 percent turnover in the principalship will result in increased numbers of women in the principalship. School district-university partnerships will be established for the purpose of early identification and preparation of aspiring principals, with a particular focus on the recruitment of minorities and women.*

With a turnover in the principalship that is projected to be as high as 56 percent by 1998, tremendous opportunities will exist for the employment of women and minorities. Also spurring this development will be continuing pressure for affirmative action programs and the increasing ethnic diversity of the nation's population. The trend revealed in the study toward wider employment of women as K-8 principals will doubtless continue and may well accelerate.

However, except for the small increase in the number of Hispanic principals revealed in this study, ground actually is being lost in the appointment of minorities of color to the elementary and middle school principalship. Moreover, this trend is likely to continue during the next decade unless aggressive minority recruitment programs are promptly initiated. This need for action is likely to stimulate the forging of new partnerships between local school districts and institutions of higher education toward identifying good prospects for administrative positions, developing individually prescribed professional development programs (including programs aimed at classroom teachers) and a wide variety of practical experiences leading to administrative internships within the school district.

2. *Principal preparation beyond the master's degree will become so common as to approach becoming standardized.*

Actually, the average preparation level of principals has been moving in this direction for the past 20 years. Meanwhile, preparation programs for teachers also are being elevated beyond the "normal" four-year bachelor's degree, and principals will need to be able to provide leadership to a more highly prepared staff.

To this mix add an apparent trend toward school site-based management and it seems likely that by the turn of the century a sixth year of preparation will become "normal" for newly hired principals.

3. *Principal preparation and inservice programs will emphasize the proficiencies necessary for site-based management, with a special focus on instructional leadership.*

With the individual school site increasingly being recognized as the focus for school improvement, the effective school principal will increasingly need to possess a broad array of administrative skills (i.e., personnel and fiscal management) as well as specific instructional leadership skills (i.e., supervision of instruction and monitoring skills for improving staff and student performance).

Further, the explosion of knowledge about teaching and learning, plus the impact that new technology is expected to exert on both instruction and management, provide additional reasons to extend principal preparation programs, as does the growing need to be knowledgeable about the operation and administration of instructional programs for three- and four-year-olds and for a rapidly expanding group of at-risk students. And beyond all these things, the study clearly indicates that principals keenly feel a need to learn how to deal more effectively with the various political forces that affect the schools these days.

It is clear that those who occupy the principalship in the coming years will be required to possess a broad array of proficiencies needed for functioning effectively both as educational leaders and as skilled managers.

Against this background, expectations are that principal preparation programs will begin to include specialized courses (and more carefully monitored practicum experiences) dealing with such areas as developmentally appropriate programs for early childhood education and meeting the needs of at-risk students. For principals already in the field, principal academies or centers will continue to grow as an inservice supplement to programs offered by school districts and universities, and by state and national professional associations.

4. *School districts will decentralize operations so that the school site is the focal point for change and accountability.*

As principals become more skilled in instructional leadership, they will be given greater freedom to make the critical decisions that affect their school. With this increased autonomy, however, will come both higher expectations and greater accountability for the results—not to speak of the possibility of performance-based administrative contracts.

These changes may be expected to have some interesting spin-offs. As principals become more autonomous, they are less likely to be moved about within a system, so that they might have more concentrated impact on the school's culture. Principals may be expected to acquire a higher level of authority and responsibility, a greater role in fiscal decision making, and an increased voice in the selection of personnel.

5. *Pressures for educational reform from the state and national levels will diminish as school administrators struggle to meet the mandates already imposed.*

The eruption of changes in elementary/middle and secondary schools touched off by publication of *A Nation At Risk* seems likely to fade, but the problems associated with some of these changes—particularly those mandated by state legislatures—will continue to challenge about 70 percent of the nation's K-8 principals.

Mandating change is relatively easy; managing the change process so that desirable improvements become a part of the school culture is much more difficult and time-consuming. Although changing the school culture is a slow process, many legislative bodies have continued to enact new mandates without waiting for full implementation of those already approved, much less for an assessment of results. Thus for a time, at least, principals will continue to be given responsibility for managing the change process and held accountable for the results.

Meanwhile, principals will become more politically astute and more adept at developing channels of communication with legislators. And as legislators are made more aware of the problems that some of their actions have inadvertently created, and as public understanding of those problems widens, the pace of mandated changes is expected to slow to a more manageable level.

6. *The collective bargaining controversy will continue to diminish in intensity and more collegial decision-making patterns to emerge.*

The emotional impact of collective bargaining as a divisive force between teachers and administrators seems to be diminishing; indeed, interest in collective bargaining itself appears to be diminishing. At the same time principals are increasingly involving the school staff in a number of decisions that affect them. This participative, collegial style seems to better "fit" the image of a profession such as teaching.

*   *   *

In providing a glimpse of the past and a summary of the present, this 1988 NAESP ten-year study also provides some optimism for the future, suggesting that if these projections are accurate, those who occupy the elementary and middle school principalship will have an increased voice in what that future will hold.

Chapter 11

The Typical K-8 Principal Today

Emerging from the data found in this report is a profile of the "typical" K-8 principal. This person is a white male, now 47 years old. He is the administrator of one school, is responsible for 472 pupils, and has been this school's principal for five years. The school staff includes 21 full-time teachers, four special area teachers, three teacher aides, and one full-time secretary. There exists in his school both a student council and some type of parent advisory council.

A professional in education for 22 years, he has been a school principal for 11 years, always in the school district he serves now. He holds a master's degree and state certification as a principal. A member of his local principal's group and his state association, he also is or has been a member of the National Association of Elementary School Principals. Although he "certainly" or "probably" would become a principal again if given the opportunity to start over, he is upwardly mobile and has aspirations that go beyond the K-8 principalship. Politically he tends to be conservative.

He has a written contract with the school district that calls for 217 days of employment (11 months) at a 1986-87 salary of $39,988. His typical work week is 45 hours plus six additional hours spent in school-related activities. His performance as an administrator is formally evaluated once each year. Secure in his job and confident of his abilities, he sees unsatisfactory student performance as his greatest potential job security problem.

He believes that he is increasingly being given authority for decisions within his school and is increasingly being held responsible for the results. Personnel evaluation, the promulgation of optimum instructional practices, and development of the curriculum are the primary areas in which his role is growing. He exercises discretionary control over 17 percent of the school budget and has at least some voice in the employment of staff within his school. All things considered, he believes the authority he is given to run his school is appropriately balanced with the degree to which he is held responsible when things go wrong.

As a group, elementary school principals are satisfied in their job, confident in their skills, and upbeat about their future.

Technical Note

Estimates of Sampling Variation

For proper use of the data contained in the summary tables in this report, the limitations of the data must be recognized. Data collected in response to *The K-8 Principal in 1988* are subject to two types of error: sampling error and nonresponse error or bias. However, only the possible error associated with sample percentages that are due to sampling variation can be estimated statistically. Table A and Table B are included to assist users of the report in drawing accurate inferences about the population, public K-8 (elementary and middle school) principals, from these sample statistics.

Confidence Intervals of Percentages

Table A provides the number of percentage points that should be added to and subtracted from an observed sample percentage in order to obtain the 90 percent confidence limits for the corresponding population. The range of percentages obtained includes the population percentage about 90 times in 100. For example, consider the sample estimate that 27.6 percent of the 834 principals feel they have much influence on school district decisions that affect elementary schools and elementary education (Table 83). To make an inference about the corresponding percentage of all K-8 principals, the following procedure should be used. Since 27.6 percent is nearer to 30 percent than any other percentage shown in the column headings of Table A, this figure is entered in the column headed 30 percent or 70

TABLE A—APPROXIMATE NUMBER OF PERCENTAGE POINTS TO BE ADDED TO AND SUBTRACTED FROM THE OBSERVED SAMPLE PERCENTAGES TO OBTAIN THE 90 PERCENT CONFIDENCE LIMITS FOR THE POPULATION PERCENTAGES

Size of subgroup	Observed percentage near				
	10% or 90%	20% or 80%	30% or 70%	40% or 60%	50%
100-199	5.0	6.6	7.6	8.1	8.3
200-299	3.5	4.7	5.3	5.7	5.8
300-399	2.9	3.8	4.4	4.7	4.8
400-499	2.5	3.3	3.8	4.0	4.1
500-599	2.2	2.9	3.4	3.6	3.7
600-699	2.0	2.7	3.1	3.3	3.4
700-799	1.9	2.5	2.9	3.0	3.1
800-899	1.7	2.3	2.7	2.9	2.9
900-999	1.6	2.2	2.5	2.7	2.7
1,000-1,099	1.6	2.1	2.4	2.5	2.6
1,100-1,199	1.5	2.0	2.3	2.4	2.5
1,200-1,299	1.4	1.9	2.2	2.3	2.4

percent. The observed percentage is based on a group of 834; therefore, the percentage appears in the row labeled 800-899. At the intersection of the designated row and column, a value of 2.7 percentage points is found. This value is subtracted from and added to the observed sample percentage in order to obtain the approximate 90 percent confidence limits that range from 24.9 to 30.3. It can be stated with 90 percent confidence that the range from 24.9 to 30.3 includes the actual percentage for all K-8 school principals, assuming nonresponse error is negligible.

Table B provides the amount of difference that can be expected between the sample percentages for subgroups of particular sizes, again assuming that nonresponse error is negligible. The table lists the approximate minimum number of percentage points by which two observed sample percentages must differ in order to infer with approximately 90 percent confidence that the corresponding population percentages are actually different. Thus, if the difference between the observed percentages exceeds the value given at the intersection of the appropriate row and column, it can be assumed with 90 percent confidence that the corresponding population percentages are different.

Consider these two sample percentages. Of the suburban principals, 18.8 percent feel they have little influence on school district decisions that affect K-8 schools and K-8 education, while 14.0 percent of small town principals express this same opinion. Is the 4.8 percentage point difference between the two groups enough to infer with approximately 90 percent confidence that a higher proportion of the population of suburban principals feel they have little influence on school district decisions that affect K-8 schools and K-8 education?

Using the higher of the two percentages as a guide, the section of Table B titled *For percentages around 20 or 80* is selected. The number of respondents from each of the two subgroups are used to determine the proper column and row. There are 200 suburban principals; therefore, the column headed 150-249 is selected. Since there are 255 small town principals, the row headed 250-349 is chosen. A value of 6.0 percentage points is found at the intersection of the appropriate row and column. Since the observed difference of 4.8 is smaller, it cannot be concluded with approx-

TABLE B—COMPARING TWO PERCENTAGES—APPROXIMATE DIFFERENCE REQUIRED FOR SIGNIFICANCE AT .90 LEVEL OF CONFIDENCE FOR SELECTED SUBGROUP SIZES

Subgroup size	Subgroup									
	50-149	150-249	250-349	350-449	450-549	550-649	650-749	750-849	850-949	950-
For percentages from 35 to 65										
50-149	11.6	10.1	9.5	9.2	9.0	8.9	8.8	8.7	8.6	8.5
150-249	10.1	8.2	7.5	7.1	6.9	6.7	6.6	6.5	6.4	6.3
250-349	9.5	7.5	6.7	6.3	6.0	5.8	5.7	5.6	5.4	5.3
350-449	9.2	7.1	6.3	5.8	5.5	5.3	5.2	5.0	4.9	4.8
450-549	9.0	6.9	6.0	5.5	5.2	5.0	4.8	4.7	4.5	4.4
550-649	8.9	6.7	5.8	5.3	5.0	4.7	4.6	4.4	4.3	4.2
650-749	8.8	6.6	5.7	5.2	4.8	4.6	4.4	4.3	4.1	4.0
750-849	8.7	6.5	5.6	5.0	4.7	4.4	4.3	4.1	3.9	3.8
850-949	8.6	6.4	5.4	4.9	4.5	4.3	4.1	3.9	3.7	3.6
950-	8.5	6.3	5.3	4.8	4.4	4.2	4.0	3.8	3.6	3.5
For percentages around 30 or 70										
50-149	10.7	9.2	8.7	8.4	8.3	8.1	8.1	8.0	7.9	7.8
150-249	9.2	7.5	6.9	6.5	6.3	6.2	6.0	6.0	5.8	5.7
250-349	8.7	6.9	6.2	5.8	5.5	5.3	5.2	5.1	5.0	4.9
350-449	8.4	6.5	5.8	5.3	5.1	4.9	4.7	4.6	4.5	4.4
450-549	8.3	6.3	5.5	5.1	4.8	4.6	4.4	4.3	4.1	4.0
550-649	8.1	6.2	5.3	4.9	4.6	4.4	4.2	4.1	3.9	3.8
650-749	8.1	6.0	5.2	4.7	4.4	4.2	4.0	3.9	3.7	3.6
750-849	8.0	6.0	5.1	4.6	4.3	4.1	3.9	3.8	3.6	3.5
850-949	7.9	5.8	5.0	4.5	4.1	3.9	3.7	3.6	3.4	3.3
950-	7.8	5.7	4.9	4.4	4.0	3.8	3.6	3.5	3.3	3.2

For percentages around 20 or 80

50-149	9.3	8.1	7.6	7.4	7.2	7.1	7.0	7.0	6.9	6.8
150-249	8.1	6.6	6.0	5.7	5.5	5.4	5.3	5.2	5.1	5.0
250-349	7.6	6.0	5.4	5.0	4.8	4.7	4.5	4.5	4.3	4.2
350-449	7.4	5.7	5.0	4.7	4.4	4.2	4.1	4.0	3.9	3.8
450-549	7.2	5.5	4.8	4.4	4.2	4.0	3.9	3.8	3.6	3.5
550-649	7.1	5.4	4.7	4.2	4.0	3.8	3.7	3.6	3.4	3.3
650-749	7.0	5.3	4.5	4.1	3.9	3.7	3.5	3.4	3.3	3.2
750-849	7.0	5.2	4.5	4.0	3.8	3.6	3.4	3.3	3.1	3.0
850-949	6.9	5.1	4.3	3.9	3.6	3.4	3.3	3.1	3.0	2.9
950-	6.9	5.0	4.2	3.8	3.5	3.3	3.2	3.0	2.9	2.8

For percentages around 10 to 90

50-149	7.0	6.0	5.7	5.5	5.4	5.3	5.3	5.2	5.2	5.1
150-249	6.0	4.9	4.5	4.3	4.1	4.0	4.0	3.9	3.8	3.7
250-349	5.7	4.5	4.0	3.8	3.6	3.5	3.4	3.3	3.3	3.2
350-449	5.5	4.3	3.8	3.5	3.3	3.2	3.1	3.0	2.9	2.8
450-549	5.4	4.1	3.6	3.3	3.1	3.0	2.9	2.8	2.7	2.6
550-649	5.3	4.0	3.5	3.2	3.0	2.8	2.7	2.7	2.6	2.5
650-749	5.3	4.0	3.4	3.1	2.9	2.7	2.6	2.6	2.4	2.3
750-849	5.2	3.9	3.3	3.0	2.8	2.7	2.6	2.5	2.3	2.2
850-949	5.2	3.8	3.3	2.9	2.7	2.6	2.4	2.3	2.2	2.1
950-	5.1	3.7	3.2	2.8	2.6	2.5	2.3	2.2	2.1	2.0

imately 90 percent confidence that the two population percentages are actually different.

Percentage points provided in both Table A and Table B do not take into account any possible nonresponse error or bias between respondents and nonrespondents to the survey, a possible source of error with both sample and nonsample surveys

TABLE C—APPROXIMATE SIZE OF SUBGROUPS IN THE 1988 NAESP TEN-YEAR STUDY OF THE PRINCIPALSHIP

Composition of Group	Number
Total Respondents	834
Sex: Male	660
Female	167
Age: 40 years or less	224
41 to 50 years	330
older than 50 years	268
Years of Experience: less than 5	171
5 to 14	367
15 or more	268
Size of School: Less than 400 students	342
400 to 600 students	299
More than 600 students	184
Community Type: Urban	187
Suburban	200
Small Town	255
Rural	178
NAESP Member: Yes	387
5 years or less	159
More than 5 years	215
No	440
Would Become a Principal Again if Starting Over:	
Certainly/probably would	679
Certainly/probably would not	133
Elementary Principalship as a Final Career Goal: Yes	363
No	434
Degree Status: Bachelor's/Master's	574
6th year/Ph.D.	244

Bibliography

A Nation At Risk: The Imperative for Educational Reform. (DOE Publication No. 065-000-00177-2). The National Commission on Excellence in Education. Washington, D.C.: U.S. Government Printing Office, 1983.

A Nation Prepared: Teachers for the 21st Century. The Carnegie Forum on Education and the Economy and the Economy's Task Force on Teaching as a Profession. New York: The Carnegie Corporation, 1986.

Bennett, William J. *First Lessons: A Report on Elementary Education in America.* (DOE Publication No. 0-161-837:QL 3). Washington, D.C.: U.S. Government Printing Office, 1986.

Blanchard, Kenneth, and Johnson, Spencer. *The One Minute Manager.* New York: The Berkley Books, 1983.

Edmonds, Ronald. *Social Policy* 7 (March/April 1979).

Effective Teachers: Effective Evaluation in America's Elementary and Middle Schools. Alexandria, Va.: National Association of Elementary School Principals, 1988.

Fringe Benefits for School Administrators in Public Schools, 1985-86. Arlington, Va.: Educational Research Service, 1986.

Hodgkinson, Harold. "What's Ahead for Education," *Principal 65* (January 1986).

Methods of Scheduling Salaries for Principals, Third Edition. Arlington, Va.: Educational Research Service, 1987.

Pharis, William L., and Zakariya, Sally Banks. *The Elementary School Principalship in 1978: A Research Study.* Arlington, Va.: National Association of Elementary School Principals, 1979.

Principal Selection Guide (DOE Publication No. IS 87-114). Washington, D.C.: U.S. Government Printing Office.

Proficiencies for Principals: Kindergarten through Eighth Grade. Standards Committee. Alexandria, Va.: National Association of Elementary School Principals, 1986.

Scheduled Salaries for Professional Personnel in Public Schools, 1987-88, Part I. Arlington, Va.: Educational Research Service, 1988.

Standards for Quality Elementary Schools: Kindergarten through Eighth Grade. Standards Committee. Alexandria, Va.: National Association of Elementary School Principals, 1984.

Teachers and Principals: May 1984 (Educator opinion poll No. 226-00001). Arlington, Va: Educational Research Service, September 1984.

The Elementary School Principalship—A Research Study. 37th Yearbook. Washington, D.C.: Department of Elementary School Principals, NEA, 1958.

The Elementary School Principalship in 1968 . . . A Research Study. Washington, D.C.: Department of Elementary School Principals, NEA, 1968.

Tomorrow's Teachers: A Report of the Holmes Group. East Lansing, Mich.: The Holmes Group, 1986.

Acknowledgments

The author is indebted to a number of organizations and individuals who contributed to the development and conduct of this study, in particular the following:

- The principals who completed the study questionnaire,
- The University of Northern Iowa, for providing me time, technological backing, and other support,
- The members of NAESP's Ten-Year Study Advisory Committee,
- Members of NAESP's Organization of Professors of Elementary School Administration,
- Educational Research Service, Inc., and particularly Nancy Protheroe and Glen Robinson,
- Joyce Broell of the Iowa Principal's Academy at the University of Northern Iowa,
- Doris Belfield, Rita Brown, Lee Goodman, Gail Gross, Ed Keller, Ellen Matthews, and Sam Sava of the NAESP staff, and finally,
- Janet Doud, my best friend and wife, who cheerfully adapted her life to the strenuous schedule required to undertake this complex project for NAESP.

James L. Doud
Director, Iowa Principals Academy